The Art of Crafting User Stories

Unleash creativity and collaboration to deliver high-value products with a delightful user experience

Christopher Lee

BIRMINGHAM—MUMBAI

The Art of Crafting User Stories

Group Product Manager: Alok Dhuri

Publishing Product Manager: Uzma Sheerin

Book Project Manager: Manisha Singh

Senior Editor: Nithya Sadanandan

Technical Editor: Maran Fernandes

Copy Editor: Safis Editing

Language Support Editor: Safis Editing

Proofreader: Safis Editing

Indexer: Rekha Nair

Production Designer: Alishon Mendonca

DevRel Marketing Coordinator: Deepak Kumar and Mayank Singh

Business Development Executive: Mayank Singh

First published: August 2023

Production reference: 1210723

Published by Packt Publishing Ltd.
Grosvenor House
11 St Paul's Square
Birmingham
B3 1R.

ISBN 978-1-83763-949-6

www.packtpub.com

To my mother, Heather Lee, for her sacrifices and for exemplifying the power of justice.

– Christopher Lee

Contributors

About the author

Christopher Lee is a product coach with a passion for helping teams deliver quality software. With over 10 years of experience, he has honed his skills in Agile methodologies, product development, and team management. Christopher has worked with start-ups and large enterprises, fostering effective collaboration and clear communication to achieve goals. He emphasizes user-centered design and values user stories as a powerful tool to clarify requirements and create value. As a skilled communicator and instructor, Christopher has a proven track record of delivering engaging coaching sessions, classes, and workshops. *The Art of Crafting User Stories* aims to share his expertise and help software professionals and teams build better software.

I want to thank the people who have been close to me and supported me, especially my mother, Heather.

About the reviewer

Ajaya Gummadi is a product leader with diverse experience in planning and executing product strategies and managing teams that drive global and scalable data transformation for enterprise customers.

She has brought database and data analytics products and solutions-as-a-service from concept to launch at Google, Amazon, and HP, partnering cross-functionally to solve complex problems for customers across industries, such as the financial, telecommunications, retail, manufacturing, and public sector industries, and drive customer acquisition, adoption, and revenue.

Ajaya encourages continued innovation in data and design through a visiting professorship and board member role at the Birla Institute of Technology and Science. She is also an advisor for BITSian-led start-ups.

Table of Contents

2

Understanding the User Perspective   19

3

Writing Effective User Stories   43

4

Prioritizing and Estimating User Stories   63

5

Working with Stakeholders   81

6

User Story Refinement and Continuous Improvement   99

7

User Stories in Practice   115

8

Expert Interviews   139

9

Conclusion   155

Index   159

Other Books You May Enjoy   168

Preface

Welcome to *The Art of Crafting User Stories*. In this comprehensive guide, we will explore the world of user stories and their pivotal role in Agile development. Whether you are a seasoned Agile practitioner or new to the methodology, this book will equip you with the knowledge and skills to effectively create, refine, and utilize user stories in your development projects.

Agile development has revolutionized the way software is built, emphasizing collaboration, adaptability, and customer-centricity. At the heart of Agile lies the concept of user stories, which capture the requirements and desired outcomes from the user's perspective. User stories enable teams to break down complex projects into manageable pieces, facilitating incremental delivery and continuous improvement, and ensuring alignment with user needs.

Throughout this book, we will delve into the core principles, techniques, and best practices for writing effective user stories. We will explore how user stories fit within the larger context of Agile development, and how they serve as a bridge between stakeholders, development teams, and end users. You will learn the art of crafting clear, concise, and actionable user stories, incorporating acceptance criteria, and effectively prioritizing and estimating them.

In addition to the fundamentals, we will also cover advanced topics such as refining user stories, continuous improvement, stakeholder management, and collaboration techniques. We will examine real-world case studies, conduct expert interviews, and provide practical examples to illustrate the concepts and techniques discussed.

By the end of this book, you will be equipped with the tools, knowledge, and insights to harness the power of user stories in Agile development. You will have a deep understanding of the user story life cycle, the benefits they bring to the development process, and the techniques to effectively implement them in your products.

So, let's embark on this journey together and master the art of user stories in Agile development!

Who this book is for

This book is for product managers, product owners, and Agile coaches that enjoy learning by doing and want to learn about writing user stories, acceptance criteria, user story splitting, Agile PRDs, estimates, and antipatterns.

What this book covers

Chapter 1, Introduction to User Stories, provides an overview of user stories and their importance in Agile software development. It starts with a definition of what user stories are and how they are used to represent the requirements and needs of end users in a product development process. In addition, the chapter sets the stage for the rest of the book by introducing key concepts and terminology that will be used throughout, such as personas, user journeys, and product backlogs.

Chapter 2, Understanding the User Perspective, covers the importance of considering end users' needs and perspectives when developing user stories. It will provide techniques for gathering and incorporating user feedback and understanding user goals, behaviors, and pain points.

Chapter 3, Writing Effective User Stories, will provide you with guidelines and best practices for writing user stories that are clear, concise, and effective. You will learn how to write user stories that accurately reflect user needs and goals and that can be easily understood by stakeholders, developers, and designers. You will also learn about the key components of a well-written user story, including the user persona, the goal, and the acceptance criteria.

Chapter 4, Prioritizing and Estimating User Stories, will cover the critical aspects of prioritizing and estimating user stories in the agile development process. You will learn how to determine the relative importance of user stories and understand the impact of user story prioritization on the overall project timeline. You will also learn how to estimate the time and resources required to complete each user story and how to incorporate these estimates into the overall product plan. Additionally, you will learn best practices for prioritizing and estimating user stories, including how to involve stakeholders in the process, how to handle changes and uncertainties, and how to monitor and adjust estimates as needed.

Chapter 5, Working with Stakeholders, focuses on the importance of involving stakeholders in the user story process. You will learn how to effectively communicate with stakeholders, including product owners, customers, and developers, to gather the information needed to write accurate and effective user stories. You will learn about techniques for eliciting requirements and involving stakeholders in the user story process, such as user story workshops and stakeholder interviews. Additionally, you will learn about the role of stakeholders in the acceptance criteria and how to involve them in the prioritization and estimation of user stories.

Chapter 6, User Story Refinement and Continuous Improvement, covers the best practices for improving the quality and effectiveness of user stories over time. You will learn about the importance of the continuous refinement and improvement of user stories and will be introduced to tools and techniques for making this process as efficient and effective as possible. Topics covered in this chapter include techniques for gathering and incorporating feedback from stakeholders, strategies for improving the clarity and specificity of user stories, and ways to keep user stories up to date and relevant as the product evolves over time.

Chapter 7, User Stories in Practice, provides hands-on guidance and practical examples of implementing user stories in real-world projects. You will learn how to apply the concepts learned throughout the book to various scenarios and see how user stories can be used to improve the development process. This chapter highlights the benefits and challenges of using user stories in practice and provides tips for overcoming common obstacles.

Chapter 8, *Expert Interviews*, will provide insights from experts in the field of user stories and requirements gathering. The chapter will highlight the experiences, best practices, and advice of these experts through a series of interviews. This chapter will also give you a sense of the challenges and opportunities that come with working with user stories in real-world scenarios.

Chapter 9, *Conclusion*, provides a summary of the key takeaways and lessons learned from the book. It highlights the importance of user stories in agile development, and you will learn about the best practices for writing and implementing effective user stories. The chapter reflects on the information presented in the book and provides insights on how to apply the knowledge in real-world scenarios. The conclusion aims to tie up loose ends and provide a clear understanding of the topic.

To get the most out of this book

You will need to understand basic web concepts but require no prior knowledge of user stories.

Conventions used

There are a number of text conventions used throughout this book.

`Code in text`: Indicates code words in text, database table names, folder names, filenames, file extensions, pathnames, dummy URLs, user input, and Twitter handles. Here is an example: "As a `[type of user], I want [a specific goal or task]` so that `[a reason or benefit for completing the goal or task]`."

Bold: Indicates a new term, an important word, or words that you see onscreen. For example, words in menus or dialog boxes appear in the text like this. Here is an example: "For example, under the **Connecting with friends** activity, user stories could include sending friend requests, accepting friend requests, and organizing friends into custom lists."

> **Tips or important notes**
> Appear like this.

Get in touch

Feedback from our readers is always welcome.

General feedback: If you have questions about any aspect of this book, mention the book title in the subject of your message and email us at `customercare@packtpub.com`.

Errata: Although we have taken every care to ensure the accuracy of our content, mistakes do happen. If you have found a mistake in this book, we would be grateful if you would report this to us. Please visit `www.packtpub.com/support/errata`, selecting your book, clicking on the Errata Submission Form link, and entering the details.

Piracy: If you come across any illegal copies of our works in any form on the Internet, we would be grateful if you would provide us with the location address or website name. Please contact us at copyright@packt.com with a link to the material.

If you are interested in becoming an author: If there is a topic that you have expertise in and you are interested in either writing or contributing to a book, please visit authors.packtpub.com.

Reviews

Please leave a review. Once you have read and used this book, why not leave a review on the site that you purchased it from? Potential readers can then see and use your unbiased opinion to make purchase decisions, we at Packt can understand what you think about our products, and our authors can see your feedback on their book. Thank you!

For more information about Packt, please visit packtpub.com.

Share Your Thoughts

Once you've read *The Art of Crafting User Stories*, we'd love to hear your thoughts! Scan the QR code below to go straight to the Amazon review page for this book and share your feedback.

https://packt.link/r/1837639493

Your review is important to us and the tech community and will help us make sure we're delivering excellent quality content.

Download a free PDF copy of this book

Thanks for purchasing this book!

Do you like to read on the go but are unable to carry your print books everywhere?

Is your eBook purchase not compatible with the device of your choice?

Don't worry, now with every Packt book you get a DRM-free PDF version of that book at no cost.

Read anywhere, any place, on any device. Search, copy, and paste code from your favorite technical books directly into your application.

The perks don't stop there, you can get exclusive access to discounts, newsletters, and great free content in your inbox daily

Follow these simple steps to get the benefits:

1. Scan the QR code or visit the link below

https://packt.link/free-ebook/9781837639496

2. Submit your proof of purchase
3. That's it! We'll send your free PDF and other benefits to your email directly

Introduction to User Stories

User stories are the backbone of the Agile development process, and they play a crucial role in creating a product that meets users' needs. In this chapter, we will cover what user stories are, their importance in the Agile process, and how to create effective user stories. By understanding the concepts covered in this chapter, you will gain a better understanding of how to use user stories to ensure that your software development product are aligned with the needs of their users. You will learn how to create user-focused stories that are easy to understand and can be completed in small iterations. Additionally, you will learn about the INVEST model and how it can be used to create effective user stories that are valuable, testable, and estimable.

If you are involved in software development, you will find this chapter particularly beneficial as it will help you to create effective user stories that meet the needs of users. By implementing the concepts discussed in this chapter, you will be able to increase your productivity and the efficiency of development, resulting in a better end product that meets the needs of users since a faster time to market increases feedback loops.

We will cover the following main topics:

- What are user stories?
- The importance of user stories in Agile
- Creating effective user stories
- A brief history and the origins of user stories
- User stories in Agile development
- Understanding the structure of a user story
- Writing user-focused and well-written user stories
- Using user stories throughout the software development life cycle
- The benefits of using user stories

What are user stories?

A user story is a short, simple description of a feature or functionality of a product that is written from the perspective of the end user. User stories are written by the product owner and are used to communicate the users' needs to the development team. The development team then uses the user stories to guide its work and create a suitable product. Next, we'll discuss the importance of user stories in Agile.

The importance of user stories in Agile

User stories are an integral part of the Agile development process. A user story is a concise, simple, and informal description of a feature or functionality from the perspective of an end user. It serves as a tool for communication and collaboration between stakeholders and the development team in the software development process. User stories are used to capture requirements, define the scope of work, and prioritize tasks in an Agile product. They were introduced as a response to the challenges of traditional requirements-gathering methods, which often involved lengthy and complex documentation that lacked clarity and failed to address the true needs of users. User stories provide a more user-centered approach, focusing on the "who," "what," and "why" of a feature, enabling better alignment between development efforts and user expectations. Agile development is an iterative approach to software development that prioritizes delivering working software frequently and responding to change quickly. User stories are used in the Agile process to break down a product into small, manageable pieces that can be completed in short iterations. A user story is a way to capture how a user will use the product or any of its features. It is written from a user's perspective in descriptive language. Collecting user stories helps us define a product. User stories also ensure that the focus of the development team is on the user's needs and not on the development team's assumptions.

Agile development has gained popularity in recent years due to its ability to produce high-quality software in a timely and efficient manner. The Agile approach involves working in short iterations or sprints, with each iteration resulting in a working software product that is delivered to the end user for feedback. User stories are a critical component of Agile development, as they help to break down a product into manageable pieces that can be completed in each sprint.

As a user, I benefit from the use of user stories in Agile development because they ensure that the product is developed in a way that meets my needs and priorities. User stories allow the development team to break down the product into smaller, manageable pieces that can be completed in each sprint. This means that I can see progress and get value from the product incrementally, rather than waiting for the entire product to be developed. User stories also enable teams to prioritize features based on user needs, ensuring that the most important functionalities are delivered early on. By using user stories, teams can continuously gather feedback from me as a user and iterate on the product, making improvements based on my input. Ultimately, user stories help create a product that is tailored to my requirements and delivers value to me as a user throughout the development process.

Here are some of the key benefits of implementing user stories:

- Ensures the focus is on the users' needs rather than on assumptions

- Facilitates communication and collaboration between stakeholders

- Provides a common language for all stakeholders involved in the development process

- Helps to ensure that everyone is on the same page regarding product goals and objectives

- Improves the efficiency of the development process

- Enables the development team to prioritize tasks based on the value they deliver to the end user

- Helps to ensure that the end user receives the maximum value from the software being developed

In summary, user stories are an essential part of the Agile development process. They help to break down a product into manageable pieces, ensure that the focus of the development team is on users' needs, facilitate communication and collaboration between stakeholders, and improve the efficiency of the development process.

The Importance of Creating Effective User Stories

Effective user stories are a key component of the Agile development process, as they provide a clear and concise way to communicate user requirements and prioritize development efforts. By following the **INVEST model**, development teams can create user stories that are **Independent, Negotiable, Valuable, Estimable, Small, and Testable**, ensuring that the end product meets the needs of the user while remaining feasible and manageable to develop. User stories are individual pieces that offer some value to the end user; are limited to an encapsulated scope that is achievable in a single sprint cycle; and can be implemented, tested, and delivered within a sprint cycle. Creating effective user stories is crucial to the success of the Agile process. A well-written user story is concise, specific, and easy to understand. Each element of the INVEST model is essential to creating an effective user story:

- **Independent**: A user story should be self-contained and not dependent on other user stories

- **Negotiable**: A user story should be negotiable, allowing for discussion and changes

- **Valuable**: A user story should deliver value to the user

- **Estimable**: You should be able to estimate the effort required for a user story

- **Small**: A user story should be small enough to be completed in one iteration

- **Testable**: A user story should be testable to ensure that it meets the users' needs

The INVEST model provides a framework for creating effective user stories. The first element of the INVEST model, **Independent**, is important because it ensures that user stories can be developed and tested without dependencies on other stories. This promotes faster development and testing cycles.

The second element, **Negotiable**, is important because it allows for discussion and changes to the scope of the user story during the development process. This flexibility is crucial in the Agile process, where requirements can change frequently.

Valuable user stories deliver value to the user. This means that the user story should have a clear benefit to the user, such as improving the user experience or increasing efficiency. A user story should meet user needs. Defining this clearly results in several benefits:

- **Alignment with user needs:** A well-defined user story ensures that the development team understands and focuses on addressing the specific needs and goals of the user. This alignment increases the chances of delivering a product that truly meets the user's requirements.

- **Improved communication and collaboration**: Clear user stories facilitate effective communication between stakeholders, including product owners, developers, designers, and testers. The shared understanding of user needs helps in collaborative decision-making and avoids misunderstandings or misinterpretations.

- **An enhanced user experience**: When user stories are defined clearly, they guide the development process toward creating functionality and features that enhance the user experience. By keeping the user's perspective in mind throughout the development cycle, the team can design and deliver solutions that are intuitive, user-friendly, and valuable.

- **An efficient development process**: Well-defined user stories enable the team to prioritize and plan their work effectively. By breaking down the requirements into smaller, manageable stories, the development process becomes more efficient, allowing for incremental delivery, faster iterations, and quicker feedback loops.

- **Increased customer satisfaction**: Clear user stories increase the likelihood of delivering a product that meets user expectations. This, in turn, leads to higher customer satisfaction and loyalty, as the user sees their needs addressed and their feedback incorporated into the product.

Overall, by defining user stories clearly, the team can ensure that the development efforts are focused on delivering value to the user, resulting in a better user experience, improved collaboration, and increased customer satisfaction.

Estimable user stories can be evaluated in terms of how much effort they will require, which is important for planning and scheduling. If user stories cannot be estimated, it can be difficult to plan and allocate resources effectively.

Small user stories should be small enough to be completed in one iteration (a single sprint). This promotes faster feedback cycles and helps the development team stay focused on delivering working software.

Finally, **Testable** user stories are important to ensure that the software meets the needs of the user. If a user story is not testable, it is difficult to determine whether the software meets user requirements.

Overall, creating effective user stories is essential to the success of the Agile development process. By following the INVEST model and ensuring that user stories are concise, specific, and easy to understand, development teams can ensure that they build software that meets users' needs.

In this section, we have covered the basics of user stories, their importance in the Agile process, and how to create effective user stories. In the next section, we will dive deeper into the anatomy of a user story and explore the different elements that make up a well-written user story.

A brief history and the origins of user stories

User stories are a powerful technique for capturing the requirements of software development products. They have been widely adopted in the Agile development community and have become an essential tool for delivering high-quality software products. This section provides an overview of how user stories have evolved over time and have become an essential tool for modern software development.

The origins of user stories

User stories were invented as a response to the traditional requirements-gathering process, which often resulted in lengthy, complex documents that were difficult to understand and did not effectively capture the needs of the end users. This process often led to misunderstandings, delays, and, ultimately, failed products.

In the late 1990s, Kent Beck, Ron Jeffries, and other software development thought leaders began to explore alternative approaches to software development that emphasized collaboration, flexibility, and customer satisfaction. This approach became known as Agile software development.

As part of this new approach, Beck and Jeffries introduced the concept of user stories as a way to capture the needs of end users simply and concisely. The idea was to focus on the user's needs and goals, rather than on technical specifications or features. User stories are intended to be a collaborative tool that fosters communication and understanding between stakeholders, developers, and users throughout the development process.

The concept of user stories was inspired by the work of Alistair Cockburn, who developed the concept of use cases in the early 1990s. Use cases were a way of describing the behavior of a system in terms of the interactions between actors and the system. While use cases provided a useful way of modeling a system, they were often considered too formal and rigid for Agile development.

User stories were intended to be a more informal and flexible alternative to use cases. Rather than focusing on the technical details of a system, user stories focused on the needs and goals of the end users. This made them easier to understand and more accessible to non-technical stakeholders, such as customers, product owners, and business analysts.

The evolution of user stories

Since its inception, user stories have been refined and adapted by many practitioners in the Agile development community. Today, user stories are a common practice in Agile methodologies such as Scrum, Kanban, and Lean. They are used by development teams around the world to capture requirements, prioritize work, and communicate with stakeholders.

One of the key factors driving the evolution of user stories has been the need to scale Agile practices to larger, more complex products. As Agile has become more mainstream, it has been applied to increasingly larger and more complex products. This has led to the development of techniques such as story mapping, which allows teams to visualize the relationships between User Stories and the larger goals of the product.

Another factor driving the evolution of User Stories has been the need to integrate them with other Agile practices such as **Acceptance Test-Driven Development (ATDD)** and **Behavior-Driven Development (BDD)**. These practices use User Stories as a starting point for defining acceptance criteria and automated tests. This helps ensure that User Stories are testable and can be verified by automated tests.

In this section, we explored the history and origins of User Stories. We saw how they were developed as a lightweight, customer-centric approach to capturing requirements, and how they have evolved over time to become an essential tool within modern software development. User Stories continue to evolve as Agile practices become more widespread, and we can expect to see further refinements and adaptations in the future. Next, we'll discuss user stories in Agile development to understand the inner components more concretely.

The importance of user stories in Agile development

Agile software development methodologies are a set of principles that prioritize flexibility, collaboration, and fast iterations in software development. The main aim of Agile development is to deliver working software frequently with the help of user feedback. One of the key aspects of Agile is to remain flexible and adaptable to changes as and when required.

User stories fit perfectly into Agile development because they provide an efficient way of capturing user requirements and prioritizing them based on their importance. User stories represent small, self-contained requirements that have business value and provide context to the development team about users' needs.

In Agile development, user stories play a vital role in defining the scope of the product, guiding the development process, and ensuring that the final product meets the needs of the users. User stories help the team to focus on the most critical features by breaking down the development process into smaller, more manageable chunks.

User stories follow a simple template:

"As a [user role], I want [feature], so that [benefit]."

This template ensures that users' needs are being addressed and that the feature has a clear user value. User stories should be written in language that can be easily understood by all members of the team, including developers, testers, and stakeholders.

The product backlog in Agile development is a prioritized list of user stories that guides the development team on what to work on next. The product owner, who represents the voice of the user, is responsible for prioritizing the backlog based on the users' needs and business value. The product owner should be available to the team to answer any questions and provide clarification on the user stories.

In **Large-Scale Scrum** (**LeSS**), backlog items are user stories, features, or any other work items that represent the work to be done by the development team. Backlog items are used to define and prioritize the work to be done, and they are organized into a product backlog and a sprint backlog. Product backlog items are higher-level items, while sprint backlog items are the items that the development team plans to complete during a sprint. The backlog items in LeSS are managed and prioritized by the Product Owner.

Once the development team starts working on a user story, they break it down into smaller tasks and estimate the effort required to complete each task. This process ensures that the development team is aligned with the users' needs and that they continuously deliver working software that meets those requirements.

In summary, user stories play a crucial role in Agile software development. They provide an efficient way of capturing user requirements, prioritizing them based on business value, and guiding the development team on what to work on next. By using user stories, Agile development teams can deliver working software frequently and ensure that the final product meets the needs of the users.

Understanding the structure of a user story

User Stories are a powerful and flexible tool for capturing requirements and communicating them to development teams. They have become an essential part of modern Agile software development methodologies, enabling teams to work collaboratively and iteratively to deliver high-quality software that meets the needs of users and stakeholders.

To effectively use User Stories, it is essential to understand their structure and the different components that make up a User Story. This section will provide an overview of the various elements of a User Story, including the three core components – the persona, the action, and the goal – and how they are used to describe the requirements and desired outcomes of a software feature or product.

Persona

The persona is the first part of a User Story and is used to describe the user or stakeholder who is the focus of the story. The persona is typically described in terms of their role, their goals, and their needs. This information is important as it helps the development team to understand who the user is and what they are trying to achieve. By understanding the persona, the team can create software that is tailored to their needs, ensuring that it is usable, accessible, and valuable.

Action

The action is the second component of a User Story and is used to describe the specific action that the user or stakeholder wants to perform. This could be anything, whether searching for information, completing a task, or making a purchase. The action should be described in clear and concise language that is easy to understand, and it should be written from the user's perspective. This helps to ensure that the team is focused on building features that are aligned with users' goals and needs.

Goal

The goal is the final component of a User Story and is used to describe the desired outcome of the user's action. The goal should be specific, measurable, and achievable, and it should be described in terms of the benefit it provides to the user or stakeholder. For example, a goal might be to increase user engagement by 10% or to reduce the time it takes to complete a task by 50%. By focusing on the goal, the team can ensure that the software they build is delivering tangible value to the user.

User stories are written in the format of "As a [user], I want [goal/desire] so that [benefit]," which is a concise and effective way to describe user requirements in software development.

"*As a*" identifies the user or persona who has a need or requirement.

"*I want*" describes the user's goal or desire.

"*So that*" explains the benefit or value that the user expects to receive.

Here's an example of a user story using this format:

As a customer, I want to be able to save my payment information so that I don't have to enter it every time I make a purchase.

This user story describes a requirement from the perspective of the customer, who wants the ability to save payment information to make future purchases more convenient. The benefit of this requirement is that it saves the customer time and makes the purchasing process smoother.

Other components

In addition to the three core components, User Stories may also include additional elements that provide additional context and detail. These may include acceptance criteria, which describe the conditions that must be met for the story to be considered complete, or epics, which are large stories that are broken down into smaller, more manageable stories.

In conclusion, User Stories are a critical part of modern software development methodologies, enabling teams to build software that meets the needs of users and stakeholders. By understanding the structure of a User Story and the different components that make it up, teams can create software that is aligned with users' goals and needs, delivering value to the user and the business. The persona, action, and goal are the core components of a User Story and should be described in clear and concise language, using the language of the user to ensure that the story is focused on their needs.

Examples of user stories for identifying and prioritizing requirements

We have discussed the structure of User Stories and their different components. We will now go through examples of User Stories and how they can be used to identify and prioritize requirements.

User Stories are an effective way to identify and prioritize requirements for software development products. They are written from the perspective of the end user and focus on the user's needs and goals. User Stories provide a clear understanding of what the user wants and why they want it. This information is then used to prioritize the features and functionality that will be developed.

Let's take a look at some examples of User Stories and how they can be used to identify and prioritize requirements:

- **Example 1 – As a frequent traveler, I want to be able to search for flights by date and destination so that I can easily find the best options for my trip**

  In this User Story, we can see that the user wants to be able to search for flights by date and destination. This is a clear requirement for the software. By prioritizing this feature, the development team can ensure that users can easily find flights that fit their needs.

- **Example 2 – As a social media user, I want to be able to share posts from other users so that I can spread the word about content that I find interesting**

  In this User Story, the user wants to be able to share posts from other users. This is a feature that will help users engage with content and share it with their own followers. By prioritizing this feature, the development team can ensure that users have a seamless experience when sharing content.

- **Example 3 – As an online shopper, I want to be able to filter products by price so that I can easily find items within my budget**

  In this User Story, the user wants to be able to filter products by price. This is a requirement that will make it easier for users to find products that fit within their budget. By prioritizing this feature, the development team can ensure that users have a positive shopping experience and are more likely to make a purchase.

These examples demonstrate how User Stories can be used to identify and prioritize requirements for software development products. By understanding the needs and goals of the end user, development teams can prioritize the features and functionalities that will provide the most value.

Writing user-focused and well-written user stories

User Stories are an essential part of Agile software development. However, not all User Stories are created equal. To be truly effective, User Stories need to be user focused and well written. In this section, we will explore why it is essential to write user-focused User Stories and how to write them.

The importance of user-focused user stories

User Stories are a way of capturing the needs and requirements of users in a succinct and easy-to-understand way. The focus of a User Story should always be on the user and their needs, rather than the technical details of the solution. This approach ensures that the development team is building software that meets the needs of end users.

When writing User Stories, it is essential to keep in mind the user's perspective. It is easy to fall into the trap of writing User Stories from the perspective of the development team or the product manager. Still, this approach can lead to User Stories that are too technical or not focused enough on user needs.

To ensure that User Stories are user-focused, it is helpful to involve end users in the process. By involving end users in the process, the development team can gain a better understanding of the users' needs and priorities.

Let's see an example of a user-focused User Story: *as a new user, I want a clear and simple onboarding process so that I can quickly understand how to use the app and start using it to manage my tasks.*

In this User Story, the focus is on the needs of a new user. The user wants to be able to quickly understand how to use the app and start managing tasks. By prioritizing a clear and simple onboarding process, the development team can ensure that new users have a positive experience and can start using the app effectively.

Here's another example of a well-written User Story: *as a sales representative, I want to be able to view my daily sales report on my mobile device so that I can quickly check my progress and adjust my strategy as needed.*

In this User Story, the requirement is specific and clearly stated. The user wants to be able to view their daily sales report on their mobile device. The reason for this requirement is also included – the user wants to be able to quickly check their progress and adjust their strategy as needed. By following the INVEST model, this User Story is concise, specific, and easy to understand.

The importance of well-written user stories

Well-written User Stories are critical for effective Agile software development. A well-written User Story should be easy to understand, concise, and contain all the necessary information. It should also be written in a way that is easy to prioritize and estimate.

A poorly written User Story can lead to misunderstandings and delays in the development process. It can also make it difficult to prioritize and estimate work accurately. To avoid these issues, it is essential to follow some best practices when writing User Stories.

One of the best practices for writing well-written User Stories is to keep them concise. A User Story should be short and to the point, containing only the necessary information. It should also be written in a way that is easy to understand and free of jargon.

Another best practice for writing well-written User Stories is to use the "*As a... I want... so that...*" structure. This structure helps to ensure that the User Story is written from the user's perspective and contains all the necessary information. It also makes it easy to prioritize and estimate work accurately.

Here's an example structure for a user-focused user story:

```
As a [type of user], I want [a specific goal or task] so that [a reason or
benefit for completing the goal or task].
```

For example:

As a customer, I want to be able to track my order status so that I can see when my package will arrive.

This structure ensures that the user's needs and goals are at the center of the story and that the development team has a clear understanding of what is needed to satisfy the user's requirements.

In conclusion, writing user-focused and well-written User Stories is essential for effective Agile software development. By focusing on the user's needs and keeping the User Stories concise and well written, the development team can build software that meets the needs of the end users. It is also essential to follow best practices for writing User Stories, such as using the aforementioned "*As a... I want... so that...*" structure. By following these best practices, the development team can ensure that User Stories are effective and easy to prioritize and estimate.

Common mistakes and pitfalls to avoid when working with user stories

User Stories can be an incredibly powerful tool when used effectively, but as with any methodology, some common mistakes and pitfalls can arise when working with User Stories. In this section, we will explore some of the most common mistakes made when using User Stories and provide guidance on how to avoid them:

- **Writing epics instead of user stories**

  One of the most common mistakes when working with User Stories is writing epics instead of User Stories. An epic is a large, high-level User Story that is often too large to be completed within a single sprint. When an epic is written instead of a User Story, it can make it difficult to plan and estimate work and can result in unclear requirements. To avoid this mistake, it is important to break down epics into smaller, more manageable User Stories that can be completed within a single sprint.

- **Not focusing on the user**

  User Stories are intended to be user-focused, but it is common for teams to lose sight of the user when creating User Stories. This can result in requirements that are not truly user-driven and can lead to software that does not meet the needs of the end user. To avoid this mistake, it is important to focus on the user and their needs when creating User Stories. Start by identifying the user, their needs, and what they hope to achieve by using the software. Keep the user at the forefront of the story and avoid getting lost in the technical details.

- **Failing to include acceptance criteria**

  Another common mistake when working with User Stories is failing to include acceptance criteria. Acceptance criteria are a set of conditions that must be met for the User Story to be considered complete. Without acceptance criteria, it can be difficult to know when a User Story is truly done, which can lead to confusion and delays. To avoid this mistake, it is important to include acceptance criteria in each User Story and make sure that they are clear and specific.

- **Not prioritizing user stories**

  When working with User Stories, it is important to prioritize them based on their importance to the user and the product. The failure to do so can result in delays and the delivery of software that does not meet the needs of end users. To avoid this mistake, it is important to prioritize User Stories based on their value to the user and the product. Consider the impact of each User Story on the end user and on the product goals and prioritize it accordingly.

- **Failing to collaborate**

  User Stories are intended to be a collaborative tool, but it is common for teams to fail to collaborate effectively when creating User Stories. This can result in misunderstandings, unclear requirements, and a lack of alignment between the development team and stakeholders. To avoid this mistake, it is important to collaborate effectively when creating User Stories. Involve all stakeholders in the process, including the development team, product owner, and end users. Make sure that everyone is aligned on the requirements and that there is clear communication throughout the process.

In conclusion, there are common mistakes and pitfalls to avoid when working with User Stories. By breaking down epics into smaller User Stories, focusing on the user, including acceptance criteria, prioritizing User Stories, and collaborating effectively, teams can avoid these mistakes and create effective User Stories that drive successful software development.

Using user stories throughout the software development life cycle

User stories are an essential part of Agile development, and they can be used in different phases of the software development life cycle. In this section, we'll discuss how user stories can be used in planning, design, and testing.

The planning phase

During the planning phase, user stories can be used to identify the features and requirements that the software needs to meet. The development team can use user stories to understand the needs and expectations of users and stakeholders. This information can then be used to create a product backlog, which is a list of features that the software needs to have. The product backlog is then prioritized based on the needs of the users and stakeholders.

The design phase

During the design phase, user stories can be used to guide the development team in creating the design of the software. The development team can use user stories to identify the different use cases and workflows that the software needs to support. This information can then be used to create the user interface and user experience for the software. By using user stories to guide the design phase, the development team can ensure that the software meets the needs of the users and stakeholders.

The testing phase

During the testing phase, user stories can be used to ensure that the software meets the needs of users and stakeholders. The development team can create test cases based on the user stories and these test cases can be used to validate the functionality of the software. By using user stories to guide the testing phase, the development team ensures that the software meets the requirements that were identified during the planning phase.

In conclusion, user stories can be used in different phases of the software development life cycle to guide the development team and ensure that the software meets the needs of the users and stakeholders. By using user stories throughout the development process, the development team can create software that is more user-focused and meets the needs of the users and stakeholders.

The role of User Stories in creating a shared understanding of product goals and objectives

One of the biggest challenges in software development is creating a shared understanding of what needs to be built. The requirements-gathering process can be time-consuming and expensive and often leads to misunderstandings between stakeholders and developers. In order to overcome these challenges, Agile software development methodologies use User Stories to create a shared understanding of a product's goals and objectives.

User Stories are a powerful tool that can help teams to better understand the needs of their users and customers. By focusing on the user's perspective, User Stories allow stakeholders and developers to identify and prioritize requirements that meet the needs of end users.

In this section, we will discuss how User Stories can be used to create a shared understanding of project goals and objectives. We will explore the benefits of using User Stories, the challenges that can arise when creating them, and how to overcome these challenges.

Benefits of using User Stories

User Stories can help teams to create a shared understanding of a product's goals and objectives in several ways. First, User Stories help to identify the needs of the end users, which can lead to better, more fitting software. Second, User Stories provide a way to prioritize requirements based on their importance to the end users. This ensures that the most important requirements are built first, which can lead to greater user satisfaction. Finally, User Stories provide a common language that can be used by stakeholders and developers to communicate with each other. This can help to avoid misunderstandings and ensure that everyone is on the same page.

User stories are an essential component of Agile software development methodologies, and they offer several benefits to the development team and stakeholders. In this section, we will discuss the benefits of using user stories in software development products. The following are some of the benefits:

- **Increased communication and collaboration**

  User stories facilitate communication and collaboration between the development team and stakeholders. In Agile development, everyone is expected to collaborate and work together toward a common goal. User stories help the team understand end users' requirements and expectations better, leading to more effective communication and collaboration. This understanding makes it easier to build software that meets users' needs, resulting in better software products.

- **Better product backlog management**

  User stories help teams manage the product backlog better. A product backlog is a list of items that need to be addressed during the development process. User stories allow stakeholders to prioritize features, which helps the development team understand the most important requirements. The team can then focus on implementing the high-priority features, which leads to a more focused development process.

- **Increased transparency**

  User stories increase transparency throughout the development process. By breaking down the product into small, manageable parts, stakeholders can understand how development is progressing better. User stories also provide visibility into what the team is working on, the current status of each feature, and any roadblocks the team is facing. With this level of transparency, stakeholders can provide timely feedback and make informed decisions, which ultimately benefits the product.

- **Improved quality**

  User stories help to improve the quality of the software product. By focusing on specific user requirements, the team can build software that meets users' needs. User stories also allow the development team to identify potential gaps and edge cases that need to be addressed, improving the quality of the final product.

- **Agile development**

  User stories are a key component of Agile development. Agile methodologies prioritize iterative development, with continuous feedback and improvement. By using user stories, development teams can break down the product into small, manageable pieces and continually refine and improve the product. This iterative process ensures that the final product meets the users' needs while allowing the team to adapt and make changes along the way.

In summary, user stories provide many benefits to development teams and stakeholders. They facilitate communication and collaboration, help manage the product backlog, increase transparency, improve quality, and are a key component of Agile development methodologies. By using user stories, development teams can build software that meets the users' needs, resulting in better software products.

Challenges when creating User Stories

Although User Stories are a powerful tool, they can be challenging to create. One of the biggest challenges is writing User Stories that are user-focused. This can be difficult for stakeholders who may not have a deep understanding of the end users. Another challenge is prioritizing requirements, as it can be difficult to determine which requirements are the most important. Finally, it can be difficult to create User Stories that are clear and concise.

Overcoming challenges when creating User Stories

To overcome these challenges, it is important to involve all stakeholders in the User Story creation process. This can help to ensure that everyone has a clear understanding of the end users and their needs. It is also important to prioritize requirements based on their importance to end users, which can be done by involving them in the prioritization process. Finally, it is important to create clear and concise User Stories that are easy to understand.

In conclusion, User Stories are a powerful tool that can help teams to create a shared understanding of product goals and objectives. By focusing on the needs of the end-users, User Stories can help to identify and prioritize requirements that meet the needs of the users. Although User Stories can be challenging to create, involving all stakeholders in the process and prioritizing requirements based on their importance can help to overcome these challenges. Ultimately, using User Stories can lead to better software that meets the needs of the end-users and satisfies stakeholders.

Summary

The chapter introduced User Stories as a tool used in Agile software development methodologies to define software requirements from the user's perspective. It discussed the history and origins of User Stories, explaining the evolution from traditional software development processes to Agile methodologies. The chapter detailed the structure of a User Story, including its components and how they work together to create a clear and concise requirement statement. It also highlighted the importance of creating well-written and user-focused User Stories and provided examples and tips for doing so. It then explained the role of User Stories in different phases of software development and how they can be used to create a shared understanding of a product's goals and objectives. It also identified common mistakes and pitfalls to avoid when working with User Stories.

Here are the skills you have gained from this chapter:

- Understanding the concept of User Stories and how they fit into Agile software development methodologies
- Knowledge of the structure and components of a well-written User Story
- The ability to create effective User Stories that are user-focused and follow the INVEST model
- Understanding the role of User Stories in different phases of software development and how they can help create a shared understanding of a product's goals and objectives

The skills and knowledge gained from this chapter will be beneficial in real life, as well as in further chapters of the book, as User Stories are a fundamental tool used in Agile software development.

Understanding how to create effective User Stories will lead to better communication and collaboration between developers and stakeholders, resulting in software that better meets user needs and expectations.

The ability to use User Stories throughout the software development process will help teams to deliver working software frequently and respond to change quickly.

Questions

1. What is the purpose of a user story in Agile development?
2. What is the INVEST model and how is it used for creating effective user stories?
3. Why is it important to keep user stories focused on users' needs?
4. What is the difference between an epic and a user story?
5. How can user stories be used in different phases of software development?

Answers

1. The purpose of a user story in Agile development is to capture a user's requirements or needs in a concise and specific manner and to ensure that the focus of the development team is on user needs and not on the development team's assumptions. User stories are used to break down a product into small, more manageable pieces that can be completed in short iterations.

2. The INVEST model is a set of criteria used to create effective user stories. It stands for Independent, Negotiable, Valuable, Estimable, Small, and Testable. Each element of the INVEST model is essential in creating an effective user story.

3. It is important to keep user stories focused on user needs to ensure that the development team is delivering value to users. By keeping user needs at the forefront of the development process, the team can create software that is useful and relevant.

4. An epic is a large user story that is too big to be completed in a single iteration. Epics are typically broken down into smaller user stories, each of which can be completed in a single iteration.

5. User stories can be used in different phases of software development, including planning, design, and testing. In the planning phase, user stories are used to define the requirements of the software. In the design phase, user stories are used to create mockups and prototypes of the software. In the testing phase, user stories are used to ensure that the software meets the users' needs.

2
Understanding the User Perspective

In today's digital age, understanding the user perspective is critical to the success of any product or service. By understanding the needs and behaviors of your users, you can create products that are tailored to their needs, resulting in higher levels of engagement, satisfaction, and loyalty.

In this chapter, we will explore understanding the user perspective in depth. We will delve into the various techniques, tools, and methodologies used to gain insights into user needs, behaviors, and motivations. You will learn how to create user personas, conduct user research, and use user data to inform product designs.

Throughout this chapter, you will gain a solid understanding of the importance of user-centric design and how it can impact the success of your products and services. You will learn how to create products that are intuitive and user-friendly and meet the needs of your target users.

In this chapter, we're going to cover the following main topics:

- Understanding the importance of user-centric design
- Creating user personas to better understand your users
- Conducting user research to gain insights into user needs and behaviors
- Analyzing user data to make informed product decisions
- Creating user journeys to improve the user experience

By the end of this chapter, you will have a comprehensive understanding of the user perspective and how to apply it to your product design process. You will be equipped with the knowledge and tools needed to create products that truly meet the needs of your users and drive engagement and loyalty.

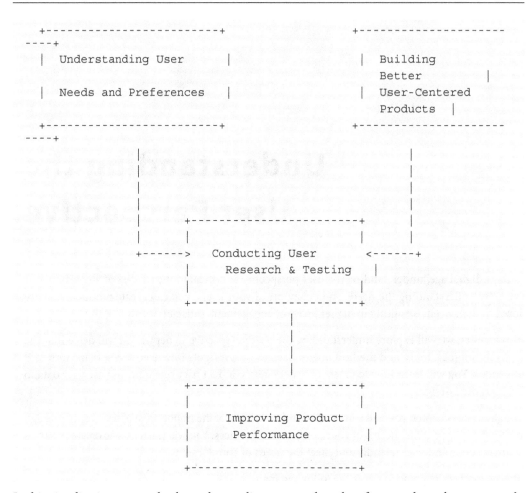

In this visualization, we see that by understanding user needs and preferences through user research, we can build better user-centered products. This results in improved product performance, leading to a more successful product.

The importance of user research

In the context of product design and development, user research refers to the process of understanding the needs, preferences, and behavior of the target users of a product or service. User research is a critical component of creating successful products because it helps ensure that the product meets the needs of its intended users.

Without user research, a product might not be designed with its users in mind, leading to poor user experiences, low adoption rates, and failed products. User research helps teams identify the features and functionality that users find valuable, as well as any pain points or areas of frustration that might need to be addressed.

In summary, user research is crucial to the success of any product development effort, as it provides valuable insights that can help shape the design and development process, leading to more successful products that meet the needs of their intended users.

Understanding user research

In today's digital age, businesses and organizations are striving to create products and services that meet the needs of their target audience. User research is an essential tool that enables businesses to understand their users and create products that meet their needs. In this section, we will explore the fundamentals of user research, including what it is, why it is important, and the various methods used to conduct user research.

In this section, we're going to cover the following main topics:

- The definition and importance of user research
- Types of user research
- The user research process
- Techniques used in user research
- The challenges and benefits of user research

The definition and importance of user research

User research is the process of collecting data about the needs, behaviors, and preferences of the target audience of a product or service. This data can be used to create products that meet user needs and provide a better user experience. User research helps businesses to understand their users, which is critical to the success of any product or service.

Types of user research

There are several types of user research that businesses can use to collect information about their target audience. Some of the most common types of user research include the following:

- **Exploratory research**: This type of research is used to explore a new or unfamiliar topic and gain a preliminary understanding of it. It often involves collecting data through interviews, surveys, or focus groups. For example, a company may conduct exploratory research to understand how consumers perceive a new product or service they are considering developing.

- **Descriptive research**: This type of research is used to describe the characteristics or behavior of a particular population or phenomenon. It often involves collecting data through surveys, interviews, or observations. For example, a researcher may conduct a survey to describe the attitudes and behaviors of a particular demographic group.

- **Experimental research**: This type of research is used to test cause-and-effect relationships between variables. It involves manipulating one or more variables and observing the effect on another variable. For example, a researcher may conduct an experiment to test the effectiveness of a new drug in treating a particular condition.

- **Observational research**: This type of research is used to observe and document behavior in a natural setting without manipulating any variables. It can involve direct observation or the use of cameras or other recording equipment. For example, a researcher may conduct observational research to understand how people use a particular public space.

- **Qualitative research**: This type of research involves collecting non-numerical data, such as opinions, attitudes, and beliefs. It often involves collecting data through interviews, focus groups, or observations. For example, a researcher may conduct qualitative research to understand how people feel about a particular social issue.

- **Quantitative research**: This type of research involves collecting numerical data, which can be analyzed using statistical methods. It often involves collecting data through surveys or experiments. For example, a researcher may conduct a quantitative survey to understand how many people use a particular product and how often they use it.

The user research process

User research typically follows a process that involves several stages, including the following:

- Identifying the objectives of the user research
- Defining the research questions
- Planning the research
- Conducting the research
- Analyzing the data
- Communicating the results

Each stage is critical to the success of user research, and the process should be followed carefully to ensure that the research is accurate and reliable. User research is a complex process that involves several stages, and following each stage carefully is crucial to ensuring accurate and reliable results. Here's a brief overview of each stage:

- **Planning**: This stage involves defining the research question, determining the research objectives, and identifying the target audience. It also involves selecting appropriate research methods and tools, creating a research plan, and defining the budget and timeline for the research.

- **Data collection**: This stage involves collecting data using various research methods, such as surveys, interviews, observations, and experiments. It's important to ensure that the data collected is relevant to the research question and objectives and that the research methods used are appropriate for the target audience.

- **Data analysis**: This stage involves analyzing the data collected to identify patterns, trends, and insights. This may involve using statistical analysis, data visualization, or other tools and techniques. It's important to ensure that the analysis is accurate, reliable, and objective.

- **Reporting**: This stage involves communicating the results of the research to stakeholders, such as product managers, designers, or executives. This may involve creating reports, presentations, or other materials that effectively communicate the research findings and insights.

- **Follow-up**: This stage involves using the research findings to inform product design and development. This may involve iterating on existing designs, developing new products, or refining marketing strategies. It's important to ensure that the research findings are integrated into the product development process and that they are used to make data-driven decisions.

By following each of these stages carefully, user researchers can ensure that their research is accurate, reliable, and effective in informing product design and development.

Techniques used in user research

There are several techniques that businesses can use to collect data about their users. Some of the most common techniques include the following:

- **Surveys and questionnaires**: Surveys and questionnaires are a useful technique for businesses that want to gather quantitative data from a large number of users. This technique can be used to collect information about user demographics, preferences, behaviors, and attitudes. This technique is suitable for businesses that have a large user base or want to gain insights about their target audience.

- **Interviews**: Interviews are a valuable technique for businesses that want to gain in-depth insights into their users' experiences, opinions, and motivations. This technique can be used to collect qualitative data from a smaller sample size. Interviews are particularly useful for businesses that are developing new products or services or want to improve their existing ones.

- **Usability testing**: Usability testing is a technique that involves observing users as they interact with a product or service. This technique is particularly useful for businesses that want to test the usability and effectiveness of their products or services. Usability testing can help businesses identify areas for improvement and make informed decisions about product design and development.

- **A/B testing**: A/B testing is a technique that involves comparing two versions of a product or service to determine which one performs better. This technique is particularly useful for businesses that want to optimize their website or app design, email marketing campaigns, or other digital assets. A/B testing can help businesses make data-driven decisions about design and content that will resonate with their users.

- **Analytics and metrics**: Analytics and metrics involve using data to track user behavior, engagement, and performance. This technique is particularly useful for businesses that want to optimize their digital marketing strategies or improve their website or app performance. Analytics and metrics can help businesses identify trends, patterns, and opportunities for improvement.

Each technique has its strengths and weaknesses, and businesses should choose the technique that best suits their needs.

Challenges and benefits of user research

User research can be a valuable tool for businesses to gain insights into their users and improve their products and services. However, there are also several challenges that businesses may face when conducting user research. Here are some of the common challenges:

- **Bias**: Bias can affect user research in several ways, such as the selection of participants, the design of the study, or the interpretation of the results. Bias can skew the data and lead to incorrect conclusions, making it important to be aware of potential biases and take steps to mitigate them.

- **Small sample size**: User research often involves recruiting a small sample size, which can make it difficult to draw generalizable conclusions. Small sample sizes can also increase the risk of bias and make it harder to identify outliers or patterns.

- **Time and resource constraints**: User research can be time-consuming and resource-intensive, especially if businesses are conducting multiple rounds of research or using multiple techniques. It may also be challenging to recruit participants or find suitable locations for testing.

- **Ethical concerns**: User research raises ethical concerns around issues such as informed consent, privacy, and confidentiality. Businesses need to ensure that they follow ethical guidelines and protect the rights and well-being of their participants.

- **Difficulty in interpreting data**: User research data can be complex and difficult to interpret, especially if the study involves multiple variables or different types of data. Businesses need to have the expertise and skills to analyze the data and draw meaningful insights.

- **Difficulty in applying insights**: Even if businesses gain insights from user research, it may be challenging to apply them effectively. Businesses need to have the resources, skills, and willingness to make changes based on the research findings.

Overall, while user research can be a valuable tool for businesses, it is essential to be aware of the challenges and take steps to address them to ensure the research is valid, reliable, and actionable.

User research can be challenging, especially for small businesses or start-ups with limited resources. However, the benefits of user research far outweigh the challenges. User research helps businesses to do the following:

- Identify user needs

- Improve the user experience

- Increase customer satisfaction

- Reduce the risk of developing a product that doesn't meet user needs

User research is an essential tool for businesses that want to create products that meet the needs of their users. It helps businesses to understand their target audience, identify their needs and preferences, and create products that provide a better user experience. By following the user research process and using the appropriate techniques, businesses can gather accurate and reliable data, which can be used to create products that meet user needs and expectations. In the next section, we will discuss personas – what they are, how they are created, and why they are an essential tool for user research. Personas are a key element of **user-centered design** (**UCD**), and they can help businesses create products and services that meet the needs and preferences of their target audience. By creating personas, businesses can gain a deeper understanding of their users and tailor their products and services accordingly. So, let's dive in and explore the world of personas!

What are personas?

Personas are a widely used design tool that helps teams understand the target audience for a product or service. Personas are fictional characters created to represent a user or group of users who share common characteristics, goals, and needs. These fictional characters help designers, developers, and stakeholders to empathize with the target audience and build products that better meet their needs.

A persona is based on research, including user interviews, surveys, and other data sources, and is designed to capture a user's goals, needs, motivations, and pain points. A persona is typically presented as a brief, one-page document that includes a name, a photo, and a brief description of the user.

In this section, we will discuss what personas are, why they are important, and how to create effective personas.

Why are personas important?

By creating personas, teams can develop a better understanding of the users' goals, needs, and behaviors. Personas help teams to create products that meet the needs of the users and are more likely to be adopted and used.

Personas also help teams to empathize with the target audience. By creating a fictional character that represents a real user, team members can put themselves in the user's shoes and understand their perspective. This understanding helps teams to create products that are more user-friendly, accessible, and engaging.

How to create effective personas

Creating effective personas involves several steps, including research, analysis, and documentation. Here are the steps to create effective personas.

Step 1 – conducting research

The first step in creating effective personas is to conduct research. This research includes user interviews, surveys, and other data sources. The goal of this research is to understand the users' goals, needs, behaviors, and pain points. The research should be conducted with a representative sample of users to ensure that the personas are accurate and representative of the target audience.

Step 2 – identifying common characteristics

The second step in creating effective personas is to identify common characteristics among the users. These characteristics can include demographic information, such as age, gender, and location, as well as psychographic information, such as values, attitudes, and behaviors. It is also the type of work done by any persona – network operator, system administrator, DBA, and so on. By identifying common characteristics, teams can create personas that accurately represent the target audience.

Step 3 – creating persona profiles

The third step in creating effective personas is to create persona profiles. Persona profiles are brief, one-page documents that include a name, a photo, and a description of the users' goals, needs, and behaviors. Persona profiles should be based on the research and common characteristics identified in the previous steps.

Here's an example of a persona profile

Name: Sarah Smith

Age: 27

Occupation: Marketing manager

Education: Bachelor's degree in marketing

Marital Status: Single

Location: Urban area

Hobbies: Yoga, traveling, cooking

Goals:

- Find a job that allows her to use her marketing skills and work in a collaborative environment

- Manage her work-life balance effectively and prioritize self-care

- Save enough money to travel to at least two new countries every year

Challenges:

- Struggles with managing her workload and often feels overwhelmed by the demands of her job

- Finds it difficult to meet new people and make friends in a new city

- Has a limited budget for travel and struggles to find affordable options

Behavior:

- Spends a lot of time researching job opportunities and networking on LinkedIn

- Likes to attend yoga classes after work to de-stress and unwind

- Enjoys exploring new neighborhoods in her city and trying out new restaurants

Note that a persona profile isn't individual/disaggregated data but aggregate data. By creating a persona profile such as this this, businesses can gain a better understanding of their users' needs, preferences, and pain points. This information can then be used to design products and services that better meet the needs of their target audience.

Step 4 – testing and refining

The final step in creating effective personas is to test and refine the personas. Testing can include user testing, where users provide feedback on the personas, as well as internal testing, where team members evaluate the personas for accuracy and usefulness. Based on the feedback, the personas can be refined to better reflect the target audience.

In conclusion, personas are a valuable tool for understanding the target audience of a product or service. By creating personas, teams can develop a better understanding of users' goals, needs, and behaviors. Personas help teams to create products that meet the needs of users and are more likely to be adopted and used. To create effective personas, teams should conduct research, identify common characteristics, create persona profiles, and test and refine the personas.

Empathy mapping – understanding users' emotions, behaviors, and motivations to improve UCD

In today's fast-paced world, it has become crucial for businesses to understand their customers and their needs. To cater to the needs of customers effectively, it is necessary to understand their pain points, desires, and motivations. **Empathy mapping** is a technique that can help businesses gain a deeper understanding of their customers. In this section, we will explore the concept of empathy mapping, its benefits, and how it can be used to create user-centric products.

What is empathy mapping?

Empathy mapping is a visual representation of a user's behavior and experiences. It is a collaborative exercise that helps teams understand their users better by putting themselves in their shoes. Empathy maps are typically created by a group of stakeholders, including product managers, designers, developers, and marketers.

Here's an example of an empathy map for a fictional user named John

Say:

"I wish this product had more features."

"I hate that it takes so long to load."

"I'm not sure whether this product is worth the price."

Do:

Visits the product website frequently

Tries to find workarounds when a feature is not available

Leaves negative reviews on social media when experiencing issues with the product

Think:

"I need a product that can keep up with my fast-paced lifestyle."

"I'm not sure whether I trust this company to deliver on its promises."

"I'm always on the lookout for better products that can improve my experience."

Feel:

Frustrated when experiencing bugs or slow loading times

Annoyed when a feature he needs is not available

Disappointed when a product doesn't meet his expectations

By creating an empathy map such as this this, businesses can gain a deeper understanding of their users' thoughts, feelings, and behaviors. This information can then be used to improve the product or service to better meet the needs and expectations of the user. For example, a business might add new features, optimize the loading speed, or adjust the pricing to address some of the pain points identified in the empathy map.

Benefits of empathy mapping

The benefits of empathy mapping are numerous. Firstly, it helps teams identify the pain points of their users, leading to the creation of more user-centric products. It also helps teams identify opportunities for innovation and the creation of new products. Empathy mapping also facilitates collaboration and communication between team members, resulting in a better understanding of the user.

Creating an empathy map

Creating an empathy map involves four steps:

1. **Identifying the user persona**: The first step is to identify the user persona that the team wants to focus on. This could be a potential customer, an existing user, or a particular segment of the user base.

2. **Collecting data**: The next step is to collect data on the user persona. This data could include their demographics, behavior patterns, motivations, desires, and pain points. This data can be gathered through user research, surveys, and interviews.

3. **Creating the empathy map**: The empathy map is typically divided into four quadrants – Says, Thinks, Feels, and Does. In each quadrant, the team members write down the thoughts, emotions, and actions related to the user persona. This can be done in a brainstorming session or through individual contributions.

4. **Analyzing the empathy map**: Once the empathy map is created, the team analyzes the data to identify patterns, insights, and opportunities. This analysis helps the team understand the user better and create user-centric products.

Empathy mapping is a powerful technique that can help businesses gain a deeper understanding of their users. By creating empathy maps, teams can identify the pain points, desires, and motivations of their users, leading to the creation of more user-centric products. The collaborative nature of empathy mapping also facilitates communication and collaboration between team members, leading to better products and happier users.

User journey mapping – understanding and optimizing the user experience across multiple touchpoints

User journey mapping is a technique that helps businesses and organizations visualize the experiences of their customers from their point of view. This technique can help identify pain points, areas of opportunity, and potential improvements that can be made to enhance the customer experience. In this section, we will explore what user journey mapping is, how it is done, and how it can benefit businesses and organizations.

We will cover the following main topics:

- What is user journey mapping?
- Why is user journey mapping important?
- How to create a user journey map
- Tips for creating effective user journey maps

What is user journey mapping?

A user journey map is a visual representation of the steps a user takes to achieve a particular goal or complete a task. It captures the customer experience, from initial contact with the product or service through the various touchpoints and interactions with the organization to the outcome. It is a detailed description of the customer's thoughts, feelings, and actions at each step of their journey.

Why is user journey mapping important?

User journey mapping is an important tool for businesses and organizations because it helps them understand the customer experience from their point of view. This understanding can help identify areas where customers may encounter difficulties, bottlenecks, or frustrations. By identifying these areas, businesses can develop solutions to address these issues, which can ultimately lead to increased customer satisfaction, loyalty, and retention.

User journey mapping can also help businesses and organizations identify opportunities to improve the customer experience. By analyzing the customer journey, businesses can identify areas where they can provide additional value or better meet the needs of their customers. This can lead to new products, services, or features that can help differentiate the business from its competitors.

How to create a user journey map

Creating a user journey map involves the following steps:

1. **Defining the customer journey**: Define the steps a customer takes to achieve a particular goal or complete a task. This may involve research, observation, or interviews with customers to understand their experience.

2. **Identifying touchpoints**: Identify the various touchpoints where the customer interacts with the organization. These may include website visits, phone calls, email, social media, or in-person interactions.

3. **Identifying customer emotions**: Identify the customer's emotions at each touchpoint. This may include frustration, satisfaction, confusion, or delight.

4. **Mapping the journey**: Create a visual representation of the customer journey, including the touchpoints and customer emotions at each step. This can be done using a template or software tools.

5. **Analyzing the map**: Analyze the map to identify pain points, areas of opportunity, and potential improvements. Typically, the CUJs also product where you would like to take the user in the future. There is a forward-looking perspective as well.

Tips for creating effective user journey maps

When creating a user journey map, consider the following tips to ensure you effectively understand and optimize the user experience across multiple touchpoints:

- **Involve stakeholders**: You start with the users before bringing in additional stakeholders. Involve stakeholders from across the organization, including customer service, marketing, and product development, to ensure a holistic view of the customer experience.

- **Keep it simple**: Focus on the key touchpoints and emotions that are most important to the customer.

- **Use visuals**: Use visuals to help tell the story of the customer journey, such as icons, images, or colors.

- **Test and iterate**: Test the user journey map with customers and iterate based on feedback to ensure accuracy and relevance.

User journey mapping is an important tool for businesses and organizations to understand the customer experience from their point of view. By identifying pain points, areas of opportunity, and potential improvements, businesses can develop solutions that can enhance the customer experience, leading to increased satisfaction, loyalty, and retention. Creating effective user journey maps involves defining the customer journey, identifying touchpoints and customer emotions, mapping the journey, and analyzing the map to identify opportunities for improvement.

Designing for the user

Designing for the user is a fundamental principle in creating products that are successful and meet user needs. When designing a product, it is important to focus on users and consider their needs, goals, and pain points. This chapter will provide an overview of the process of designing for the user and the key principles and methods involved.

In this section, we will cover the following topics:

- UCD
- Design thinking
- User research
- Usability testing
- Accessibility
- Mobile-first design

UCD

UCD is an approach to design that focuses on the needs and requirements of the user. The goal is to create a product that is easy to use and meets the needs of the user. The process involves understanding the user, their needs, and their goals and designing a product that meets those needs.

Design thinking

Design thinking is an approach to problem-solving that puts the user at the center of the process. Design thinking involves empathizing with the user, generating ideas, prototyping solutions, and testing them to ensure they meet the user's needs. The process begins with gaining a deep understanding of the user's needs and pain points, then brainstorming and ideating potential solutions. The next step is to create prototypes and test them with users, iterating and refining them until the final product is a solution that truly addresses the user's needs.

User research

User research involves gathering data about users and their needs. This data can be collected through interviews, surveys, and observation. The goal of user research is to gain insights into the users' behavior, motivations, and pain points, which can then be used to inform the design of the product.

Usability testing

Usability testing involves observing users as they interact with a product to identify areas of difficulty or frustration. The goal is to gather feedback on the usability of the product and identify areas for improvement. Usability testing can be conducted through in-person testing, remote testing, or automated testing.

Accessibility

Accessibility involves designing products that are usable by people with disabilities. This includes designing for visual impairments, hearing impairments, motor impairments, and cognitive impairments. Accessibility can be achieved through design techniques such as color contrast, text size, and alternative text for images.

Mobile-first design

Mobile-first design is an approach to design that prioritizes designing for mobile devices first, and then scaling up for larger screens. The goal is to create a product that is optimized for mobile devices, which are increasingly the primary way that users access the internet. Mobile-first design involves designing for smaller screens, simplified navigation, and fast load times.

Designing for the user is a critical component of creating successful products. UCD, design thinking, user research, usability testing, accessibility, and mobile-first design are all important principles and methods to consider when designing for the user. By focusing on the user and their needs, designers can create products that are intuitive and easy to use and meet user expectations.

Designing for the user – a comprehensive guide

Designing a product that truly meets the needs of its users requires a deep understanding of those users' needs, preferences, and pain points. In this section, we'll explore the key principles and best practices for designing with the user in mind. From conducting user research to creating empathy maps and user journey maps, we'll cover the tools and techniques you need to gain a comprehensive understanding of your users and create products that truly meet their needs. Whether you're a product designer, developer, marketer, or business owner, this guide will help you design with empathy and create products that delight your users.

Principles of user-centered design

Designing for the user requires a deep understanding of users' needs, preferences, and behaviors. To create products that satisfy users and meet their expectations, designers need to apply UCD principles throughout the design process. UCD is a framework that emphasizes involving users in the design process to create products that are functional, usable, and enjoyable. In this section, we will discuss the key principles of UCD and how they can be applied to designing products that meet users' needs.

Principle 1 – user involvement

This means engaging users in every stage of the design process, from research and ideation to testing and evaluation. By involving users in the design process, designers can gain insights into users' needs, preferences, and behaviors, which can inform the design of products that meet their needs. User involvement can take many forms, including interviews, surveys, usability testing, and co-design sessions.

Principle 2 – focusing on user goals and tasks

Designers should start by understanding users' goals and tasks and design products that support them. User goals and tasks should be the driving force behind the design process, and designers should continually evaluate design decisions based on how well they support users' goals and tasks. This principle emphasizes the importance of designing products that are goal-oriented, rather than feature-oriented.

Principle 3 – design for usability

Usability refers to how easy it is for users to use a product to accomplish their goals. Designers should aim to create products that are easy to learn about, efficient to use, and error-free. To design for usability, designers should conduct usability testing throughout the design process to identify and address usability issues. They should also follow established usability guidelines and best practices to ensure that products are usable.

Principle 4 – striving for accessibility

Accessibility refers to how easy it is for people with disabilities to use a product. Designers should aim to create products that are accessible to as many people as possible, including people with disabilities. To design for accessibility, designers should follow established accessibility guidelines and best practices, such as the **Web Content Accessibility Guidelines** (**WCAG**). They should also involve people with disabilities in the design process to gain insights into their needs and preferences.

Principle 5 – consistency

Consistency refers to how consistent a product's design is across different contexts and situations. Consistency helps users learn how to use a product more quickly and reduces the cognitive load required to use it. Designers should aim to create products that are consistent in their design and behavior across different contexts, such as different screens or platforms. They should also follow established design patterns and standards to ensure consistency.

Principle 6 – design for context

Context refers to the situational factors that influence how a product is used, such as the user's environment, task, and device. Designers should aim to create products that are tailored to their users' context to maximize their usability and effectiveness. To design for context, designers should conduct contextual research to gain insights into how users interact with products in different situations. They should also design products that are adaptable to different contexts and situations.

Principle 7 – iteration and feedback

UCD is an iterative process that involves testing and refining designs based on feedback from users.

Design sprints

Design sprints are a time-bound, structured approach to solving complex problems and developing new ideas. They provide a framework for cross-functional teams to work together and rapidly prototype and test potential solutions. Design sprints can be used to improve existing products, develop new products, or solve organizational challenges.

In this section, we will discuss the steps involved in a typical design sprint and how to implement one effectively.

Introduction to design sprints

Design sprints were first introduced by **Google Ventures** (**GV**) as a five-day process for teams to quickly identify and solve complex problems. The methodology has since been adopted by many organizations and has evolved into various forms, ranging from three-day to 10-day sprints.

The goal of a design sprint is to rapidly prototype and test ideas to reduce the time and cost associated with product development. Design sprints help teams to align on a common goal and develop solutions that are user-centered and data-driven.

The design sprint process is typically conducted by a cross-functional team that includes members from design, product, engineering, marketing, and other relevant departments. The team collaborates to develop a prototype that can be tested with users, providing feedback to refine and improve the solution.

Phases of a design sprint

Design sprints typically have five phases – Understand, Define, Sketch, Decide, and Prototype:

1. **Understand**: In the first phase, the team develops a common understanding of the problem they are trying to solve. This involves conducting user research, reviewing data, and analyzing existing solutions. The goal is to identify user pain points, generate insights, and develop a shared understanding of the problem.

2. **Define**: In the second phase, the team defines the problem they are trying to solve, identifies the user's needs, and develops a problem statement. The problem statement is critical to ensuring that the team is aligned and focused on solving the right problem.

3. **Sketch**: In the third phase, the team generates multiple ideas to solve the problem. This phase is typically done through individual brainstorming, followed by group discussions and critiques. The goal is to generate as many ideas as possible and to identify the best solutions.

4. **Decide**: In the fourth phase, the team selects the best idea to move forward with. This involves analyzing the pros and cons of each idea and making a group decision on which idea to prototype.

5. **Prototype**: In the final phase, the team develops a low-fidelity prototype of the chosen solution. The prototype is designed to be tested with users, providing feedback to refine and improve the solution.

Tips for a successful design sprint

Here are some tips to ensure that your design sprint is successful:

- **Define a clear problem statement**: The problem statement should be specific, measurable, and aligned with the users' needs.

- **Invite the right people**: The team should be cross-functional and include members from different departments, with diverse perspectives and expertise.

- **Time-box each phase**: Each phase of the design sprint should be time-boxed to ensure that the team stays focused and productive.

- **Test with real users**: The prototype should be tested with real users to get feedback on the solution and identify areas for improvement.

- **Iterate and refine**: The design sprint is just the beginning. The team should use the feedback from testing to iterate and refine the solution.

Design sprints are a valuable tool for product teams to rapidly prototype and test potential solutions. They provide a structured approach to solving complex problems and help teams to align on a common goal. By following the five phases of a design sprint and implementing the tips for success, teams can develop user-centered and data-driven solutions that meet the needs of their users.

Understanding the user perspective and diversity and inclusion

In the world of design, understanding the user perspective is critical to creating products and services that meet their needs. However, it's not enough to design for just one type of user. To truly create products that are usable and accessible to all, designers must consider diversity and inclusion in their design process. In this section, we'll explore how understanding the user perspective and diversity and inclusion intersect, and how to design products that are inclusive of all.

The benefits of designing for diversity and inclusion

Diversity and inclusion in design are important because they help ensure that products and services are usable for and accessible to everyone. When designers design with diversity and inclusion in mind, they create products that are accessible to a wider range of people, including those with disabilities or from different cultural backgrounds. Designing for diversity and inclusion has numerous benefits, including the following:

- **Increased accessibility**: When designers consider diversity and inclusion in their design process, they are creating products that are accessible to more people, including those with disabilities

- **Increased usability**: Designing for diverse users ensures that the product is usable by a wider range of people, regardless of their background or experience

- **Improved user satisfaction**: When a product is designed with the needs of diverse users in mind, it is more likely to meet their needs and increase user satisfaction

- **Expanded customer base**: Designing for diverse users means that a product can appeal to a wider range of people, increasing the potential customer base

- **Improved brand reputation**: By designing for diversity and inclusion, companies can show that they value all their customers, regardless of their background or ability

Designing for diversity and inclusion

Designing for diversity and inclusion involves several key considerations:

- **Understanding different perspectives**: To design for diverse users, designers must understand the different perspectives of those users. This involves conducting research to understand the needs and preferences of users from different backgrounds.

- **Considering accessibility**: Designers must also consider accessibility when designing for diverse users. This includes ensuring that the product is accessible to people with disabilities and designing for different cultural and language preferences.

- **Avoiding stereotypes**: Stereotypes can be harmful and exclusionary. Designers must avoid using stereotypes in their designs and instead focus on creating products that are inclusive and welcoming to all.

- **Testing with diverse users**: Testing the product with a diverse group of users is important to ensure that it meets the needs of all users.

- **Providing multiple options**: Providing multiple options can help ensure that the product is accessible to a wider range of users. This includes providing different language options or accessibility options.

Designing for the user perspective and diversity and inclusion go hand in hand. By understanding the needs of diverse users and designing products that are accessible and inclusive, designers can create products that meet the needs of all users. The benefits of designing for diversity and inclusion are numerous, including increased accessibility, usability, and user satisfaction. It's time for designers to consider diversity and inclusion in their design process to create a more inclusive world.

Understanding the user perspective and unconscious bias

Designing for the user is essential for creating successful products and services. To design effectively, it is important to understand the user perspective and avoid unconscious bias. This section will explore what unconscious bias is, how it affects design, and strategies to overcome it.

What is unconscious bias?

Unconscious bias refers to attitudes or beliefs that are automatically activated and influence a person's behavior and decisions without their awareness. Everyone has unconscious biases, which are often based on social and cultural stereotypes. These biases can influence the way we interact with others, make decisions, and design products and services.

How unconscious bias affects design

Unconscious bias can lead to products and services that are not inclusive or accessible to all users. Designers may unknowingly create products that cater to their own biases, rather than the needs and perspectives of diverse users. For example, a team of designers may create a mobile app that is optimized for right-handed users, without considering left-handed users. This bias can lead to the exclusion of left-handed users who may find the app difficult or impossible to use.

Strategies to overcome unconscious bias in design include the following:

- **Awareness**: The first step in overcoming unconscious bias is to become aware of it. Designers should examine their own beliefs and assumptions and consider how they may influence their design decisions. This can be done through self-reflection, training, and education.

- **User research**: Conducting user research is essential for understanding the needs and perspectives of diverse users. Designers should ensure that research is conducted with a diverse group of participants and that their perspectives are taken into account during the design process.

- **Diversity and inclusion**: Design teams should strive to create a culture of diversity and inclusion. This includes ensuring that diverse voices are heard and represented on the team, creating a safe and inclusive workspace, and actively seeking out diverse perspectives during the design process.

- **Testing and feedback**: Designers should test their products and services with diverse users and seek feedback. This can help identify any biases that may have been missed during the design process and ensure that the final product is inclusive and accessible to all users.

Designing for the user requires an understanding of the user perspective and a commitment to diversity and inclusion. Unconscious bias can have a significant impact on design decisions, but by becoming aware of bias, conducting user research, creating a culture of diversity and inclusion, and testing and seeking feedback, designers can create products and services that are inclusive and accessible to all users.

The role of user feedback

One of the most important ways to gain an understanding of the user perspective is to seek out feedback from users themselves. This feedback can come in many forms, such as surveys, user interviews, or usability testing. By gathering this feedback, designers can gain insights into how users interact with their products and identify areas for improvement.

However, it's important to be mindful of the limitations of user feedback. Users may not always be able to articulate their needs and preferences or may be influenced by factors such as social desirability bias (the tendency to give answers that are seen as socially acceptable). Additionally, user feedback can sometimes be contradictory or confusing, making it difficult to know which changes to prioritize.

To address these challenges, it's important to approach user feedback with a critical eye and to use multiple sources of data to inform design decisions. This may include analyzing usage data to see how users are actually interacting with a product, conducting user research to gain deeper insights into user needs and motivations, and testing design changes with real users to see how they respond.

The importance of iteration

Designing for the user perspective is an ongoing process that involves continuous iteration and improvement. Even the most well-designed products will require updates and changes over time as user needs and preferences evolve.

One key to successful iteration is to incorporate user feedback and data into the design process. This can help ensure that changes are aligned with user needs and preferences and can help identify areas for improvement that may not be immediately apparent.

However, it's also important to strike a balance between incorporating user feedback and maintaining a clear design vision. Sometimes, users may request changes that are not in line with the overall design goals or may not be feasible given technical constraints. In these cases, it's important to weigh user feedback against other factors, such as business goals, technical feasibility, and design principles.

Ultimately, designing from the user perspective is about balancing the needs of users with the constraints of the design context. By being mindful of user needs and preferences, and by using feedback and data to inform design decisions, designers can create products that are both user-centered and effective in achieving their goals.

Summary

Understanding the user perspective is crucial for designing products that meet user needs and expectations. This chapter discussed several important topics related to UCD, including user research, personas, empathy mapping, user journey mapping, and design sprints.

The chapter began with an introduction to UCD, which emphasizes the importance of focusing on user needs throughout the design process. It then discussed the importance of user research and the various methods that can be used to gather information about user needs, preferences, and behaviors.

The chapter also explored the use of personas to create UCDs that take into account the needs and goals of different user groups. Empathy mapping and user journey mapping were also discussed as tools for gaining a deeper understanding of user needs and behaviors.

Design sprints were introduced as a collaborative and time-bound process for quickly prototyping and testing design ideas.

Finally, the chapter explored the important topic of diversity and inclusion in UCD. It discussed the potential impact of unconscious bias on design decisions and the importance of designing for a diverse range of users to ensure that all users are able to access and use products and services.

Overall, this chapter highlighted the importance of understanding the user perspective in designing effective products and services that meet the needs and expectations of diverse user groups. By following a UCD approach and being mindful of unconscious biases, designers can create products that are accessible, inclusive, and effective for all users. In the next chapter, we will explore the key components of effective user stories

Questions

1. What is the user perspective?
2. Why is understanding the user perspective important?
3. What are some methods for gathering information about the user perspective?
4. What are some common challenges to understanding the user perspective?
5. How can designers and developers incorporate the user perspective into their work?

Answers

1. The user perspective is the viewpoint of the person who is using a product or service. It encompasses their goals, needs, preferences, challenges, and operations.

2. Understanding the user perspective is important because it helps designers and developers create products that meet the needs of their intended users. It can also help identify areas where the user experience can be improved.

3. Some methods for gathering information about the user perspective include conducting user research, analyzing user feedback, creating user personas, and observing user behavior.

4. Common challenges in understanding the user perspective include bias, assumptions, and a lack of empathy for the user's experience. It can also be difficult to accurately interpret user feedback and behavior.

5. Designers and developers can incorporate the user perspective into their work by involving users in the design process, conducting user testing, creating UCD solutions, and continually gathering feedback from users. They can also use user research to inform design decisions and prioritize features based on user needs.

3

Writing Effective User Stories

User stories are a crucial component of the Agile methodology and are used to define requirements from the user's perspective. Writing effective user stories can ensure that a product is focused on meeting user needs and can result in a successful product. In this chapter, we will discuss the importance of user stories in the design and development process, and how to write effective user stories. We will cover the following main topics:

- The anatomy of a user story
- Best practices for writing user stories
- Acceptance criteria: Ghkerin
- How to write effective user stories
- Common mistakes to avoid when writing user stories
- Best practices for using user stories in Agile development

The anatomy of a user story

User stories are a powerful tool for capturing and communicating requirements in Agile software development. They are short, simple descriptions of a feature or functionality from the perspective of the user. To create an effective user story, you need to understand its anatomy. Each user story consists of three key elements:

- **Persona**: This is the prime target, audience, user, or customer who will benefit from and use the feature or functionality being developed. The persona should be clearly defined and specific to the story. It should include details such as the user's name, role, and any relevant demographic information.

- **Action**: This is the specific action that the persona wants to perform. It should be clear and concise and written in the active voice. The action should describe what the user wants to do, not how they want to do it.

- **Goal**: This is the outcome that the persona wants to achieve by performing the action. The goal should be specific, measurable, achievable, relevant, and time specific and should describe the value that the feature or functionality will provide to the user.

Here's an example of a user story that includes all three elements:

"As a customer, I want to be able to save items to my shopping cart so that I can purchase them later without having to search for them again."

In this example, the persona is a customer, the action is to save items to their shopping cart, and the goal is to make it easier for them to purchase items in the future without having to redo the search (hence saving time).

In addition to these three key elements, user stories may also include acceptance criteria, which describe the conditions that must be met for the story to be considered complete. Acceptance criteria should be specific and measurable and should provide a clear definition of what is required for the story to be considered done.

By understanding the anatomy of a user story, you can create effective user stories that capture the needs and goals of your users and drive development forward effectively.

Acceptance criteria in user stories

Acceptance criteria are an essential component of a user story, as they outline the specific conditions that must be met for the story to be considered complete. By defining acceptance criteria, the development team and stakeholders can agree on the expected outcome of the user story and ensure that it meets the needs of the end user.

In this section, we will discuss the importance of acceptance criteria in user stories and provide best practices for writing effective acceptance criteria.

Importance of acceptance criteria

Acceptance criteria are important for several reasons:

- **Clear expectations**: Acceptance criteria define the expected outcome of a user story in clear, measurable terms. This helps the development team and stakeholders agree on what success looks like and ensures everyone is on the same page.

- **Testable criteria**: Acceptance criteria provide a clear set of testable criteria that the development team can use to verify that the story has been completed successfully.

- **Quality assurance**: Acceptance criteria provide a way to ensure that the product meets the required quality standards.

- **Prioritization**: Acceptance criteria help prioritize user stories by identifying the most important requirements and ensuring that they are met first.

Best practices for writing acceptance criteria

Writing clear and effective acceptance criteria is crucial for ensuring that user stories are well defined and can be properly tested. By following best practices for writing acceptance criteria, you can enhance the quality of your user stories and improve the overall success of your software development products. In this section, we will explore some key best practices to consider when crafting acceptance criteria that are specific, measurable, achievable, relevant, and time-bound. These practices will help you create acceptance criteria that effectively capture the desired outcomes and enable accurate testing and validation:

- **Use clear, concise language**: Acceptance criteria should be written in clear, concise language that is easy to understand. Avoid using technical jargon or complicated language that could be misunderstood.

- **Be specific**: Acceptance criteria should be specific and measurable. Use measurable data, such as numbers, dates, and so on, to define the expected outcome of the story.

- **Focus on the end user**: Acceptance criteria should focus on the needs of the end user. Ensure that the criteria outline the user's requirements and preferences.

- **Keep it simple**: Acceptance criteria should be simple and easy to understand. Avoid adding unnecessary complexity or detail that could lead to confusion.

- **Be realistic**: Acceptance criteria should be realistic and achievable. Avoid setting unrealistic expectations or requirements that cannot be met.

- **Include negative scenarios**: Acceptance criteria should also include negative scenarios or edge cases. This helps ensure that the user story works in all possible scenarios and that any potential issues are identified and addressed.

- **Collaborate with stakeholders**: Acceptance criteria should be developed collaboratively with stakeholders, including the end user. This ensures that everyone is on the same page and that the criteria reflect the user's needs and preferences.

In conclusion, acceptance criteria are a critical component of a user story, as they define the specific conditions that must be met for the story to be considered complete. By following these best practices, development teams can write effective acceptance criteria that meet the needs of the end user, ensure high-quality outcomes, and prioritize user stories effectively.

How to write effective user stories

When writing user stories, it is important to consider the following questions: *Who is the user? What is their goal? Why is this goal important to them? What are the acceptance criteria for the user story?* These questions will help you create user stories that are concise, clear, and effective.

Let's look at some key points that will help you write effective user stories:

- **Focus on the user**: User stories are all about the user's needs and goals. Keep the user at the center of your focus while writing a user story.

- **Keep it simple**: A user story should be brief, simple, and easy to understand. It should not include technical jargon or unnecessary details.

- **Use a standard format**: Use a standard format, such as the *"As a [user], I want [goal], so that [reason]"* format, to ensure consistency across all user stories.

- **Avoid ambiguity**: Ambiguity in a user story can lead to confusion and misinterpretation. Make sure the story is clear and unambiguous, and avoid using vague or unclear language.

- **Include acceptance criteria**: Include clear acceptance criteria that define what needs to be done for the user story to be considered complete.

- **Keep the user story independent**: User stories should be independent of one another, meaning that they should not depend on other stories to be completed. This makes it easier to prioritize and schedule the stories and ensures that the development team can work on them in any order.

- **Prioritize user stories**: Prioritize user stories based on the user's needs and the value they bring to the product.

- **Refine and iterate**: Refine and iterate the user stories as you learn more about the user's needs and goals.

- **Use user stories as a conversation starter**: User stories are not meant to be a detailed specification but rather a conversation starter. Use them to start a conversation between the development team and the user and refine the story based on their feedback.

Effective user stories are crucial in Agile methodology as they ensure the product meets the user's needs and goals. To achieve this, it's important to focus on the user, keep it simple, use a standard format, include acceptance criteria, prioritize user stories, and refine and iterate. These practices lead to a shared understanding of what is being built and why, ultimately resulting in a successful product.

In conclusion, user stories are a critical component of Agile development, and following these best practices can help ensure that they are effective and focused on delivering value to the user. By starting with the user, keeping it simple, using the right format, making it specific, using personas, prioritizing and estimating, collaborating with stakeholders, and continuously refining, development teams can create user stories that drive the development of high-quality software that meets the needs of the user.

Common mistakes to avoid when writing user stories

User stories are a wonderful way to capture user needs and requirements in an Agile development process. However, writing effective user stories can be challenging, and there are common mistakes that many teams make. In this section, we will discuss some of the most common mistakes to avoid in order to author better stories.

There are several common mistakes that can be made when writing user stories. These are included in the following list:

- **Focusing on implementation details**: One of the most common mistakes when writing user stories is focusing too much on implementation details. User stories should focus on what the user wants to achieve, not how it will be implemented. Avoid adding implementation details in the user story. Instead, leave the implementation details for the development team to decide.

- **Writing user stories that are too broad or too narrow**: User stories should be written in such a way that they capture a user's need. However, it's easy to write user stories that are too broad or too narrow. A broad user story doesn't provide enough context for the development team, and a narrow user story can be too prescriptive. Avoid these issues by ensuring your user stories are focused on one specific user need or requirement.

- **Failing to capture acceptance criteria**: Acceptance criteria are the specific conditions that must be met for the user story to be considered complete. Failing to capture acceptance criteria can lead to misunderstandings between the development team and stakeholders. Ensure that each user story includes clear and concise acceptance criteria.

- **Not involving the right stakeholders**: Writing effective user stories requires input from various stakeholders, including users, customers, and **subject matter experts** (**SMEs**). Not involving the right stakeholders can lead to incomplete or inaccurate user stories. Involve the relevant stakeholders in the user story-writing process to ensure the stories accurately capture user needs and requirements.

- **Forgetting about non-functional requirements**: Non-functional requirements are the characteristics of the system that don't relate to specific user needs but are still essential for the system's success. Examples include performance, security, and scalability. Don't forget to include non-functional requirements in your user stories, as they can have a significant impact on the system's success.

- **Writing vague user stories**: User stories that are too vague can be difficult to understand and may not provide the necessary context for the development team. Avoid vague user stories by ensuring that each story is clear, concise, and specific.

- **Failing to prioritize user stories**: Prioritizing user stories per sprint is critical to the success of the development process. Failing to prioritize user stories can lead to wasted time and resources. Ensure that each user story is prioritized based on its importance to the user and the overall product.

- **Writing user stories in isolation**: Writing user stories in isolation can lead to stories that don't align with the product's overall goals and objectives. Involve the development team, users, SMEs, and other stakeholders in the user story-writing process to ensure that each story aligns with the overall product goals.

- **Failing to revisit user stories**: User needs and requirements can change throughout the development process. Failing to revisit user stories regularly can lead to stories that are no longer relevant or accurate. Ensure that user stories are revisited and updated regularly as part of backlog refinement to reflect changes in user needs and requirements.

In conclusion, writing effective user stories requires focus, collaboration, and attention to detail. Avoiding these common mistakes can help ensure that your user stories accurately capture user needs and requirements and lead to a successful development process.

There are several differences between a requirements document and user stories in terms of structure, focus, level of detail, and collaborative nature. Here are the key distinctions:

- **Structure**: A requirements document typically follows a structured format, providing detailed specifications, diagrams, and technical requirements. User stories, on the other hand, are concise, informal narratives written from the user's perspective.

- **Focus**: Requirements documents often focus on capturing comprehensive system requirements, including functional and non-functional aspects. User stories, however, prioritize the user's needs and goals, focusing on the value delivered to the user.

- **Level of detail**: Requirements documents tend to be highly detailed, covering various aspects of the system, such as **user interface** (**UI**) design, database schema, and integration requirements. User stories, in contrast, are intentionally kept at a high level and capture the essence of the user's requirement.

- **Collaborative nature**: Requirements documents are often created by business analysts or product managers and handed off to the development team. User stories, on the other hand, encourage collaboration between the development team and stakeholders, promoting a shared understanding and eliciting valuable feedback.

- **Iterative and Agile approach**: User stories are commonly used in Agile development methodologies, where requirements evolve over time. They are designed to support an iterative and incremental approach to software development. In contrast, requirements documents are typically associated with more traditional, waterfall-style methodologies.

- **Flexibility**: User stories provide flexibility in prioritization and allow for changes and reprioritization based on evolving user needs. Requirements documents, being more detailed and rigid, may require significant effort to modify or update.

It's important to note that user stories and requirements documents can be used together or in combination, depending on the product and team's needs. The choice between the two approaches often depends on the development methodology, the product's complexity, and the level of collaboration desired with stakeholders.

Concrete examples of writing effective user stories

Understanding how to write effective user stories is essential for driving successful software development products. In this section, we will delve into concrete examples that illustrate the key principles and elements of well-crafted user stories. These examples will provide practical insights and demonstrate how to apply the concepts discussed earlier in the chapter. By examining real-world scenarios and dissecting the components of user stories, you will gain a deeper understanding of how to create user stories that are clear, concise, and aligned with the needs and goals of your users. Through these concrete examples, you will be able to strengthen your user story writing skills and enhance your ability to communicate requirements effectively to your development team.

Example 1 – user story for an e-commerce website

As a customer, I want to be able to filter my search results by price, brand, and category so that I can quickly find the products I'm interested in.

This user story is effective because it clearly states the user's goal, which is to *find products quickly*. It also specifies the criteria the user wants to use to filter their search results. The story is written in a concise and straightforward format, making it easy for the development team to understand the requirements.

Example 2 – user story for a mobile app

As a commuter, I want to be able to access real-time transit information, including bus and train schedules, so that I can plan my journey and avoid delays.

This user story is effective because it provides a clear understanding of the user's goal, which is to *access real-time transit information*. It also specifies the type of information the user wants to access, which includes bus and train schedules. The story is written from the user's perspective, making it easier for the development team to empathize with the user's needs.

Example 3 – user story for a social media platform

As a user, I want to be able to see the number of likes and comments on my posts so that I can gauge the popularity of my content and adjust my strategy accordingly.

This user story is effective because it provides a clear understanding of the user's goal, which is to *gauge the popularity of their content*. It also specifies the type of information the user wants to access, which includes the number of likes and comments. The story is written in a concise and straightforward format, making it easy for the development team to understand the requirements.

Example 4 – user story for a product management tool

As a product manager, I want to be able to assign tasks to team members, set due dates and priorities, and track progress so that I can ensure that products are completed on time and within budget.

This user story is effective because it provides a clear understanding of the user's goal, which is to *manage products effectively*. It also specifies the type of tasks the user wants to assign, including setting due dates and priorities. The story is written from the user's perspective, making it easier for the development team to empathize with the user's needs.

Example 5 – user story for a healthcare app

As a patient, I want to be able to schedule appointments with my healthcare provider, access my medical records, and receive notifications for upcoming appointments so that I can manage my health effectively.

This user story is effective because it provides a clear understanding of the user's goal, which is to *manage their health effectively*. It also specifies the type of information the user wants to access, including medical records and upcoming appointments. The story is written in a concise and straightforward format, making it easy for the development team to understand the requirements.

Effective user stories are essential for Agile software development. They help the development team understand the user's needs and requirements, which in turn leads to the development of better products. In this section, we have provided some concrete examples of effective user stories. These examples demonstrate how to write user stories that are concise, specific, and written from the user's perspective. By following these examples, you can ensure that your user stories are effective and lead to the development of high-quality products.

Including negative and edge cases in your user stories is important to ensure comprehensive testing and accounting for potential error scenarios. Here are some examples of how you can include them:

1. **Identify negative and edge cases**: Consider scenarios where the user may encounter errors, exceptions, or uncommon situations. These cases typically involve inputs or conditions that deviate from the expected or ideal flow.

2. **Write user story variations**: Create separate user story variations for negative and edge cases, highlighting the specific scenario or condition you want to address. These variations should focus on capturing the specific user need and the desired outcome, even in challenging situations.

3. **Describe acceptance criteria**: Define acceptance criteria for each user story variation, describing the expected behavior, error handling, or special conditions. Be clear and specific about what should happen in these cases, including any error messages, system responses, or alternative paths.

4. **Collaborate with the team**: Discuss the negative and edge cases with your development team, testers, and other stakeholders to ensure a shared understanding. Their input can help refine the scenarios and identify additional cases that may need consideration.

5. **Prioritize and estimate**: Include the negative and edge case user stories in your product backlog, prioritizing them alongside other user stories. Estimate the effort required to address these cases, considering their complexity and potential impact on the system.

By explicitly including negative and edge cases in your user stories, you promote a more comprehensive approach to testing and ensure that your product can handle various scenarios and user interactions effectively.

Here are some examples of negative and edge cases and their corresponding acceptance criteria for a user story:

- **User story**: *As a user, I want to reset my password in order to regain access to my account*

  Negative case: The following defines the negative case acceptance criteria for this user story:

  - When the user enters an invalid email address for a password reset, an error message should be displayed indicating that the email address is invalid

  - If the user enters an email address that is not associated with any account, an error message should be displayed stating that no account is found with the provided email address

  - When the user enters an email address that is associated with an account but has not been verified, an error message should be displayed instructing the user to verify their email before proceeding with the password reset

  - If the user's account has been locked due to multiple failed login attempts, an error message should be displayed informing the user to contact support for assistance with the password reset

  Edge case: The following defines the edge case acceptance criteria for this user story:

  - When the user enters a password that does not meet the minimum complexity requirements (e.g., length, special characters), an error message should be displayed indicating the specific requirements for a valid password

  - If the user tries to reset their password multiple times within a short period, a temporary lockout period should be implemented to prevent abuse and protect the user's account

  - When the user successfully resets their password, they should be redirected to the login page with a success message confirming the password reset

These examples showcase how acceptance criteria can help identify and address negative cases, ensuring that the user story covers various scenarios and user interactions.

Avoid ambiguity in user stories

Ambiguity in user stories can lead to confusion and misinterpretation, which can cause delays in development, rework, and even product failure. In order for user stories to be effective, they must be clear and unambiguous. This section will explore how to avoid ambiguity in user stories and ensure that they accurately convey the requirements and desired outcomes of a software feature or product.

Define terminology

One of the most common sources of ambiguity in user stories is the use of unclear or unfamiliar terminology. It is important to define any technical terms or industry-specific jargon in the user story to ensure that everyone on the development team has a clear understanding of the requirements. This can be achieved by including a glossary of terms in the user story or by providing definitions within the story itself.

Use clear language

In addition to defining terminology, it is important to use clear and concise language in user stories. Avoid using complex sentence structures or overly technical language that may be difficult for team members to understand. Instead, use simple, straightforward language that clearly communicates the requirements and desired outcomes of the feature or product.

Eliminate ambiguity

Ambiguity in user stories can lead to misunderstandings and misinterpretations, resulting in development delays and product failure. To avoid ambiguity, it is important to be specific and detailed in the user story. Use concrete examples and avoid vague or general statements that can be interpreted in multiple ways.

Consider all scenarios

When writing a user story, it is important to consider all possible scenarios that the user may encounter when using the software feature or product. This includes both positive and negative scenarios, such as error messages or unexpected outcomes. By considering all possible scenarios, the user story can be written in a way that accurately reflects the requirements and desired outcomes of the feature or product.

Collaborate with stakeholders

Collaborating with stakeholders is an important step in avoiding ambiguity in user stories. By involving stakeholders in the development process, you can ensure that the user story accurately reflects their needs and expectations. Stakeholders can also provide feedback on the clarity and effectiveness of the user story, helping to identify any potential sources of ambiguity.

Use acceptance criteria

Acceptance criteria are a set of requirements that must be met in order for the user story to be considered complete. By including acceptance criteria in the user story, you can ensure that the requirements are clearly defined and unambiguous. Acceptance criteria should be specific and measurable and include any necessary technical details or constraints.

Test the user story

Testing the user story is an important step in ensuring that it is clear and unambiguous. This can be done by reviewing the story with other members of the development team or by creating a prototype or mockup of the feature or product. Testing can help identify potential sources of ambiguity or confusion, allowing you to make revisions before development begins.

Use templates

Using templates can help to ensure consistency and clarity in user stories. Templates can be customized to include specific requirements and desired outcomes, as well as acceptance criteria and technical details. By using a template, you can ensure that all necessary information is included in the user story and that it is written in a clear and concise manner.

Avoiding ambiguity in user stories is essential for the success of any software development product. By defining terminology, using clear language, eliminating ambiguity, considering all scenarios, collaborating with stakeholders, using acceptance criteria, testing the user story, and using templates, you can ensure that your user stories accurately convey the requirements and desired outcomes of the feature or product. By following these best practices, you can help to ensure the success of your software development product and deliver high-quality software that meets the needs of your users.

Keep the user story independent

In Agile development, user stories are an essential tool for breaking down a product into manageable pieces and delivering a quality product that meets the user's needs. One of the key principles of writing effective user stories is to keep them independent of one another.

What does it mean for a user story to be independent? It means that each story should stand alone and not depend on any other story to be completed. This allows the development team to work on the stories in any order, making it easier to prioritize and schedule them.

There are several reasons why keeping user stories independent is important. Let's look at some of them here:

- **Easier to prioritize**: When user stories are independent, they can be prioritized based on their importance to the user and the overall product. This makes it easier for the product owner to decide which stories to work on first and which can be put lower down the development priority.

- **Increases flexibility**: When user stories are independent, they can be worked on in any order and by multiple teams. This provides more flexibility in the development process and allows the team to adapt to changing requirements or unforeseen challenges.

- **Reduces dependencies**: When user stories are dependent on each other, it creates a web of dependencies that can make it difficult to manage the product. This can lead to delays and make it harder to deliver a quality product.

- **Encourages collaboration**: When user stories are independent, it encourages collaboration between team members. Each team member can work on their assigned stories without worrying about dependencies on other team members.

To keep user stories independent, it's important to ensure that each story is clear and well defined. This means that the story should have a clear goal, a defined persona, and a specific action or task to be completed.

It's also important to avoid including dependencies within the user story. Dependencies can be introduced when a story is too broad or too vague. For example, a user story that reads, *"As a user, I want a search function so that I can find what I'm looking for,"* is too broad and could be broken down into the following smaller, more specific stories:

- *As a user, I want to be able to search for products by name so that I can find specific items quickly*

- *As a user, I want to be able to filter my search results by category, price, and other criteria so that I can narrow down my search*

- *As a user, I want to see suggested search terms as I type in the search box so that I can easily find what I'm looking for*

- *As a user, I want to be able to save my search results and return to them later so that I don't have to repeat the search process*

Another way to avoid dependencies is to make sure that each user story is focused on a single feature or requirement. If a story includes multiple requirements, it may be difficult to complete without depending on other stories.

In summary, keeping user stories independent is a key principle in Agile development. It allows for easier prioritization, increases flexibility, reduces dependencies, and encourages collaboration. By ensuring that each user story is clear and well defined and avoiding dependencies, development teams can deliver a quality product that meets the user's needs in a timely and efficient manner.

Scrum encourages the elimination of dependencies as much as possible. The framework suggests that teams should aim to be as self-organizing as possible and avoid relying on other teams or individuals to complete their work. This approach can increase productivity, reduce delays, and improve the overall quality of the product. Scrum provides various techniques for dependency elimination, such as reducing the scope of work, simplifying the design, or organizing work in a way that minimizes inter-team dependencies. However, in some cases, dependencies may be necessary, and in those cases, Scrum recommends managing them through regular communication and collaboration between teams to ensure the smooth progress of the product.

Use user stories as a conversation starter

User stories are an excellent tool for facilitating communication and collaboration between the development team and the users. They provide a shared understanding of what the users need and how the software feature or product can meet those needs.

One of the key benefits of user stories is that they are not meant to be detailed specifications. Instead, they are meant to be a conversation starter. Use user stories as a starting point for a conversation between the development team and the users, and refine the story based on their feedback. This can help to ensure that the software feature or product meets the user's needs and expectations.

Here are some tips for using user stories as conversation starters:

- **Start with the user**: Begin by focusing on the user and their needs. This helps to ensure that the story is grounded in real-world requirements rather than technical or organizational constraints.

- **Use plain language**: Use plain, non-technical language to describe the user story. Avoid using technical jargon or acronyms that the user may not understand.

- **Keep it simple**: User stories should be simple and straightforward. Avoid overcomplicating the story with unnecessary details.

- **Use visual aids**: Visual aids, such as diagrams or wireframes, can help to illustrate the user story and facilitate the conversation.

- **Encourage feedback**: Use the user story as a starting point for a conversation, and encourage feedback from the users. This can help to refine the story and ensure that it meets their needs and expectations.

By using user stories as a conversation starter, software development teams can ensure that they are building software that meets the user's needs and expectations. It can also help to build trust and collaboration between the development team and the users, leading to a better product.

Job stories

Job stories, also known as **Jobs-to-be-done** stories, are a valuable tool in the world of product development and user-centered design. Coined by Clayton Christensen and further popularized by Alan Klement and Bob Moesta, job stories provide a framework for understanding and addressing the needs of users in a specific context.

Unlike user stories that focus on features and functionality, job stories shift the perspective to the underlying motivations and desired outcomes of users. They capture the *job* that users are trying to accomplish when they engage with a product or service. A job story typically follows a simple structure –

When [situation], I want to [motivation], and so I can [expected outcome].

The structure of a job story encourages a deeper understanding of user needs by considering the specific context in which the job arises, the motivation driving the user to perform the job, and the expected outcome or benefit they seek to achieve. This helps teams empathize with users and design solutions that effectively address the users' needs.

Job stories are particularly valuable in uncovering user goals and motivations that may not be immediately obvious through traditional requirement-gathering methods. They focus on the broader context and emotional aspects of a user's experience, going beyond the functional aspects of a product or service.

In practice, job stories can be used as a collaborative tool during product discovery and design phases. They provide a shared language and framework for product teams, designers, and stakeholders to align their understanding of user needs and guide decision-making throughout the development process.

When creating job stories, it is essential to involve a diverse range of perspectives, including users and subject matter experts, to ensure a comprehensive understanding of the problem space. By continuously refining and iterating job stories, teams can better prioritize features, design experiences that meet user expectations, and ultimately deliver products that satisfy the underlying motivations and goals of their users.

Overall, job stories provide a valuable complement to user stories by capturing the broader context and motivations behind user interactions. They help teams gain a deeper understanding of user needs, enabling them to build more meaningful and effective solutions. By incorporating job stories into practice, product teams can enhance their user-centered approach and increase the likelihood of creating products that truly meet the needs and expectations of their target audience.

Key strategies to address the downsides

Mitigating the downsides of user stories is crucial to ensure that the resulting product or service meets the needs and expectations of users effectively. Two key strategies for addressing these downsides are conducting thorough persona research and mapping and validating assumptions.

- **Persona Research**: Personas are fictional representations of specific user archetypes or segments, and they provide valuable insights into users' goals, motivations, behaviors, and pain points. Conducting in-depth persona research helps teams develop a deeper understanding of their target users. By investing time in persona research, teams can mitigate the following downsides of user stories:

  - **Lack of user empathy**: User stories can sometimes be written without a genuine understanding of the user's perspective. Persona research helps teams empathize with users by uncovering their needs, preferences, and context. This empathy enables teams to create more relevant and user-centric user stories.

  - **Incomplete or inaccurate user stories**: Without proper user research, user stories may miss important details or make incorrect assumptions about users. Persona research provides a foundation for crafting accurate and comprehensive user stories that reflect the diverse range of user needs and behaviors.

- **Unaddressed user pain points**: Persona research allows teams to identify pain points and challenges faced by users. By integrating these insights into user stories, teams can focus on addressing these pain points and delivering solutions that truly alleviate user frustrations.

- **Assumption mapping and validation**: User stories are often based on assumptions about users, their needs, and the solutions required. To mitigate the risks associated with assumptions, teams can adopt the following practices:

  - **Assumption mapping**: Teams should explicitly identify and document the assumptions underlying user stories. This includes assumptions about user behaviors, motivations, and preferences, as well as assumptions about the feasibility and effectiveness of proposed solutions. Mapping assumptions helps teams recognize potential gaps in their understanding and serves as a basis for further investigation and validation.

  - **Assumption validation**: Teams should actively seek opportunities to validate their assumptions through user research, feedback loops, and iterative testing. User interviews, usability testing, surveys, and analytics data can provide valuable insights for validating or disproving assumptions. This iterative validation process allows teams to refine user stories based on real user feedback and ensure that the final product or service meets user expectations.

By incorporating thorough persona research and assumption mapping/validation into their process, teams can address the downsides of user stories effectively. These practices enable teams to develop a deeper understanding of users, align their assumptions with user realities, and create user stories that accurately reflect user needs and motivations.

Concrete examples of job stories

Job stories are a valuable tool in user-centered design and product development, helping teams gain a deeper understanding of user motivations and needs. They provide a structured framework for capturing the context, motivation, and expected outcome of user interactions with a product or service. Here, we will explore some concrete examples of job stories to illustrate how they can be applied in practice:

- Example 1: ordering food via delivery service

  When I'm feeling hungry after a long day at work (situation), I want to easily order food online (motivation) so that I can enjoy a delicious meal without the hassle of cooking or going out (expected outcome).

- Example 2: planning a vacation

  When I have vacation time coming up (situation), I want to research and book a holiday destination (motivation) that offers relaxation, adventure, and cultural experiences (expected outcome).

- Example 3: managing personal finances

  When I receive my monthly paycheck (situation), I want to track my expenses and create a budget (motivation) to ensure financial stability and savings (expected outcome).

- Example 4: fitness tracking

  When I go for a run (situation), I want to track my distance, pace, and calories burned (motivation) to monitor my progress, set goals, and maintain a healthy lifestyle (expected outcome).

These examples highlight how job stories capture the user's situation, their motivation, and the desired outcome. They provide a clear focus on the user's context, needs, and goals, allowing product teams to better empathize with users and design solutions that meet their specific requirements.

It's important to note that job stories should be specific, actionable, and outcome oriented. They should avoid prescribing a particular solution or technology and instead focus on the user's underlying needs and the value they seek to gain from using the product or service.

By leveraging job stories, product teams can align their efforts with user needs, prioritize features effectively, and deliver solutions that truly resonate with their target audience. These concrete examples demonstrate the practical application of job stories and their ability to guide the development of user-centered products and services.

Ultimately, this leads to the development of more successful and user-centered products or services. In the following section, we will delve into the fascinating world of story mapping, exploring its dynamic utility in designing and shaping stories, and illustrating its transformative impact on the way we conceive and convey stories.

Story mapping

Story mapping is a valuable technique used in Agile product development to visualize and organize user stories into a coherent and meaningful narrative. It provides a holistic view of the product's functionality and helps teams understand the user journey from end to end. By creating a story map, teams can mitigate several challenges and enhance collaboration and alignment among team members. The following explains the concept and benefits of story mapping.

Story mapping – creating a visual narrative

Story mapping is a collaborative exercise that involves arranging user stories in a hierarchical and sequential manner to represent the user's experience and the flow of the product's features. It typically involves two dimensions:

- Horizontal axis that represents the user's workflow or journey
- Vertical axis that represents the priority or level of detail for each user story

To create a story map, teams begin by identifying the high-level activities or user goals. These activities are placed on the horizontal axis as the backbone of the map. Then, teams break down each activity into smaller, actionable user stories, which are placed vertically beneath their corresponding activity. The map evolves as more user stories are added, forming a comprehensive and structured representation of the product's functionality.

Benefits of story mapping

Story mapping is a powerful technique in Agile product development that helps teams gain a holistic view of their product and plan its delivery effectively. By visually representing the user journey and organizing user stories, story mapping offers several key benefits that enhance collaboration, improve prioritization, and ensure a better understanding of user needs. In this section, we will explore the various advantages of story mapping and how it contributes to successful product development.

- **Visualization and clarity**: Story mapping provides a visual representation of the entire product journey, helping teams gain a clear understanding of the product's scope and the relationship between different features and user activities. It allows teams to see the big picture and identify any gaps or missing functionalities.

- **User-centric approach**: Story mapping encourages teams to think from the user's perspective. By organizing user stories based on the user journey, teams can better empathize with users and ensure that the product delivers a seamless and meaningful experience.

- **Sequencing and prioritization**: The vertical arrangement of user stories in a story map enables teams to prioritize features and functionality based on their importance and value to the user. It helps teams identify the **minimum viable product** (**MVP**) and establish a clear roadmap for iterative development.

- **Alignment and collaboration**: Story mapping promotes collaboration among cross-functional team members. It brings together individuals from different roles, such as product owners, designers, developers, and testers, to collectively understand and contribute to the product's narrative. It encourages discussions, feedback, and alignment around the user's needs and goals.

- **Iterative development and adaptability**: Story maps are dynamic and flexible tools that can evolve throughout the product development lifecycle. As the team gains insights and feedback from users and stakeholders, they can adapt and adjust the story map accordingly – adding or modifying user stories to reflect changing priorities or requirements.

- **Communication and stakeholder engagement**: Story maps serve as effective communication tools for sharing the product vision and progress with stakeholders. They provide a clear representation of the product's functionality and help stakeholders understand the rationale behind feature prioritization and sequencing.

By leveraging story mapping techniques, teams can overcome challenges related to understanding user needs, sequencing features, and fostering collaboration. It helps them create a shared understanding of the product's direction and facilitates the development of a user-centered and value-driven product.

Example of concrete story maps

Story mapping is a powerful technique for visualizing the user journey and organizing product features in a meaningful way. Here's an example of a concrete story map for a product management software:

Objective: To create a product management software that helps teams collaborate effectively and track progress.

Story map

1. **Epic: User registration and onboarding**

   - User story: As a new user, I want to create an account and set up my profile.

   - User story: As a new user, I want to receive a welcome email with instructions on getting started.

   - User story: As a new user, I want to complete a guided tour of the software's key features.

2. **Epic: product creation and setup**

   - User story: As a product manager, I want to create a new product and define its scope.

   - User story: As a product manager, I want to assign team members to the product and set their roles.

   - User story: As a product manager, I want to establish product milestones and deadlines.

3. **Epic: Task management**

   - User story: As a team member, I want to view my assigned tasks and their due dates.

   - User story: As a team member, I want to update the status of my tasks (in progress, completed, etc.).

   - User story: As a team member, I want to collaborate with other team members on task-related discussions.

4. **Epic: Progress tracking and reporting**

   - User story: As a product manager, I want to visualize the progress of tasks and milestones.

   - User story: As a product manager, I want to generate reports on product status and team performance.

   - User story: As a product manager, I want to receive notifications for overdue tasks or potential bottlenecks.

5. **Epic: Integration and Customization**

   - User story: As a user, I want to integrate the software with popular product management tools (e.g., Jira, Trello).

   - User story: As a user, I want to customize the software's interface and dashboard to match my preferences.

   - User story: As a user, I want to receive timely updates and announcements from the software's development team.

This example demonstrates how a story map organizes user stories into logical epics and their associated tasks. It provides a visual representation of the user journey from onboarding to product creation, task management, progress tracking, and customization. By laying out the features in this way, the team gains a clear understanding of the product's scope and the user's perspective, enabling them to prioritize and develop the software incrementally.

The story map serves as a collaborative tool for the entire team, fostering discussions, refining requirements, and keeping everyone aligned with the overall product vision. It allows for flexibility and adaptability as the team iterates and adds or modifies user stories based on user feedback and changing needs.

Summary

This chapter on *Writing Effective User Stories* has covered the fundamental principles and best practices for creating user stories that are clear, concise, and effective. You will have gained a deeper understanding of the following key points that help to create a successful user story:

- What user stories are and how they are used in software development
- The benefits of using user stories in Agile development
- The key components of a user story, including the persona, action, and goal
- How to avoid ambiguity in user stories by using clear and unambiguous language
- The importance of keeping user stories independent and not dependent on other stories
- How to use user stories as a conversation starter to facilitate collaboration and feedback
- Best practices for writing user stories, such as focusing on user needs and keeping stories small and manageable
- The role of acceptance criteria in defining the success criteria for a user story

By mastering these principles and best practices, you will be able to create user stories that accurately capture user needs, facilitate communication and collaboration between stakeholders, and drive the development of high-quality software products that meet the needs of end users.

Effective user stories are a key component of successful Agile development. They help to keep the focus of the product on the user's needs and goals, prioritize requirements and features, and ensure that everyone on the team is working towards the same goal. When writing user stories, it is important to focus on the user's perspective, be specific and measurable, and avoid common mistakes. By following best practices for using user stories in Agile development, teams can create successful products that meet the needs of their users.

In the next chapter, we will cover prioritizing and estimating user stories.

Questions

1. What are user stories?

2. Why are user stories important in Agile development?

3. What are some common mistakes to avoid when writing user stories?

4. How can you ensure that user stories are well written and effective?

5. How can you prioritize user stories in Agile development?

6. How do you measure the success of user stories in Agile development?

7. How can user stories be adapted to fit different types of products or development methodologies?

8. How can user stories be used to facilitate collaboration and communication within Agile teams?

9. How can user stories be used to drive innovation in Agile development?

Answers

1. User stories are brief, simple descriptions of a feature or function of a software application written from the perspective of the end user.

2. User stories help Agile teams focus on delivering value to the end user and enable them to plan and prioritize development work based on the needs of the user.

3. Some common mistakes include writing overly complex or technical stories, failing to specify acceptance criteria, and focusing on the solution rather than the problem.

4. It's important to involve stakeholders and end users in the story writing process, use clear and concise language, and focus on the user's goals and needs rather than the technical details of the solution.

5. Prioritization can be based on a variety of factors, including the user's needs and goals, the business value of the feature, the effort required to implement it, and the risk associated with delaying or not implementing it.

6. Success can be measured by how well the feature meets the needs of the user, how much business value it delivers, and how well it integrates with other features in the product.

7. User stories can be adapted to fit different product types or methodologies by adjusting the level of detail, using different formats or templates, and tailoring the language and terminology to the specific context.

8. User stories can be used as a starting point for discussions between developers, testers, and other stakeholders and can help to ensure that everyone is on the same page regarding the user's needs and goals.

9. User stories can be used to encourage teams to think creatively and develop new and innovative ways to meet the user's needs, while still delivering value and staying within the constraints of the product.

4

Prioritizing and Estimating User Stories

Prioritizing helps the development team to focus on the most valuable features or functionality, while estimating provides an approximation of how long it will take to complete a given story. These activities are essential for effective product planning, resource allocation, and stakeholder communication. In this chapter, we will focus on prioritizing and estimating user stories, which are important activities in Agile software development.

We're going to cover the following main topics:

- Understanding the importance of prioritizing and estimating user stories
- Techniques for prioritizing user stories, including MoSCoW and value-based prioritization
- **Weighted Shortest Job First (WSJF)**
- **Reach, Impact, Confidence, and Effort (RICE)** and the Kano model
- Approaches for estimating effort, including story points and ideal days
- Factors to consider when estimating, such as complexity
- Factors to consider when estimating, such as cycle time, lead time, and throughput
- Best practices for effective prioritization and estimation in Agile development products
- The #NoEstimates movement
- Concrete examples of prioritizing and estimating user stories

By the end of this chapter, you will have a clear understanding of how to prioritize and estimate user stories in an Agile development environment. You will have learned about the key principles and techniques used to identify and rank stories based on their business value and how to estimate the effort required to complete them. You will also have gained insight into the common challenges associated with these activities and how to overcome them to ensure successful product outcomes.

Chapter prerequisites

To follow along with the examples and exercises in this chapter, you will need a basic understanding of Agile software development principles and the Scrum framework. You will also need a tool or software that supports user story prioritization and estimation, such as Jira, Trello, or Pivotal Tracker.

It is also recommended to have a team of at least two people participating in the prioritization and estimation exercises. Additionally, familiarity with Agile estimation techniques, such as story points or T-shirt sizing, will be helpful.

Understanding the importance of prioritizing and estimating user stories

In Agile software development, prioritizing and estimating user stories is an essential step to ensure successful product delivery. Prioritization ensures that the most important features are delivered first, while estimation helps in planning and allocating resources. In this section, we will discuss the importance of prioritizing and estimating user stories and how these tasks can help in achieving the product goals.

Why is prioritization important?

Prioritizing user stories is essential because it helps the team to focus on the most important features and deliver them first. Prioritization also helps with managing the product scope, minimizing risk, and maximizing the value delivered to customers. It can be done based on the following factors:

- Business value
- User feedback
- Technical complexity
- Product timelines

Business value

Prioritizing user stories based on business value helps to deliver the most valuable features first. Business value can be measured in terms of revenue, customer satisfaction, and **return on investment** (**ROI**). The team can work with the product owner to identify the features that will provide the highest business value and prioritize them accordingly.

User feedback

Prioritizing user stories based on user feedback is crucial because it ensures that the product meets the user's expectations. The team can gather user feedback through various methods, such as user surveys, user interviews, and usability testing. The team can use this feedback to identify the features that are most important to the users and prioritize them accordingly.

Technical complexity

Prioritizing user stories based on technical complexity helps to manage product risks and ensures that the most technically challenging features are delivered first. The team can identify the features that require the most technical effort and prioritize them accordingly.

product timelines

Prioritizing user stories based on product timelines helps to ensure that the product is delivered on time. The team can use product timelines to identify the features that need to be delivered first and prioritize them accordingly. This ensures that the most critical features are delivered first and the product is delivered on time.

Why is estimation important?

Estimating user stories is important because it helps in planning and allocating resources. Estimation helps to determine the amount of time and effort required to deliver a feature. This helps the team to plan and allocate resources accordingly. Estimation also helps in identifying product risks and managing them effectively.

Estimating user stories can be done using various techniques, such as Planning Poker, T-shirt sizing, and the Bucket system:

- **Planning Poker** is a popular technique used by Agile teams. In Planning Poker, the team estimates the effort required to complete a feature using a deck of cards with different values

- **T-shirt sizing** is a technique where the team estimates the size of a feature using T-shirt sizes such as XS, S, M, L, and XL

- The **Bucket system** is a technique where the team categorizes the features into buckets based on the amount of effort required to deliver them

Prioritizing and estimating user stories is an essential step in Agile software development. By prioritizing and estimating user stories effectively, Agile teams can ensure product success and deliver value to customers.

Techniques for prioritizing user stories, including MoSCoW and Value-based prioritization

There are several techniques that Agile teams can use to prioritize user stories. Two of the most popular techniques are **MoSCoW prioritization** and **Value-based prioritization**.

MoSCoW prioritization

MoSCoW prioritization is a technique used to prioritize user stories based on their level of importance. **MoSCoW** stands for **Must Have**, **Should Have**, **Could Have**, and **Won't Have**.

Must Have

These are the critical stories that are necessary for the product to be considered complete. Compromises can't be made on these features and they must be delivered within the scheduled timeframe.

Should Have

These features are important but not critical. They are desirable and should be included, if possible, but if they are not delivered within the scheduled timeframe, they can be postponed to a later release. Usually, a workaround exists if the story cannot be implemented in a particular release.

Could Have

These features are nice to have but not necessary. They can be delivered if time and resources permit, but if not, they can be dropped without affecting the overall product vision.

Won't Have

These are features that are not feasible, practical, or aligned with the overall product vision. They should be dropped from the product backlog and not considered for implementation.

Value-based prioritization

Value-based prioritization is a technique used to prioritize user stories based on their business value. This technique involves assigning value to each user story based on the benefits it provides to the business. The value can be assigned in various ways, such as by calculating the ROI or using a scoring system.

Here are some steps to perform value-based prioritization:

1. **Identify the business objectives**: The first step is to identify the business objectives that the product aims to achieve. These objectives should be aligned with the overall product vision and mission.

2. **Define the metrics**: Next, define the metrics that will be used to measure the business value. These metrics could be financial, such as revenue or cost savings, customer acquisition, or churn, or non-financial, such as customer satisfaction or user engagement.

3. **Assign values to user stories**: Assign values to each user story based on how well it helps achieve the business objectives and the defined metrics. For example, a user story that helps increase customer retention could be assigned a higher value than a user story that adds a minor feature.

4. **Prioritize the backlog**: Sort the user stories in the product backlog based on their assigned values. Start with the highest-value stories and work down the list.

Prioritizing user stories is a critical aspect of Agile development. It helps ensure that the team is focused on delivering the most valuable features first and that the product vision is aligned with the business objectives. MoSCoW prioritization and Value-based prioritization are two popular techniques for prioritizing user stories. The team should choose the most appropriate technique based on their product requirements and objectives. The following are various prioritization techniques that can be employed depending on the product's needs and goals:

- **MoSCoW**: Best suited for products where there are clear "must-haves" and "nice-to-haves" that can be easily distinguished. It's also useful when there are constraints on resources, time, or budget.

- **Value-based prioritization**: Ideal for products that require maximizing value and ROI, particularly when there are many competing features or requirements.

- **RICE**: Useful for products where impact and reach are essential factors. For example, if the goal is to drive user adoption or increase revenue, this technique could help determine which features will have the most significant impact.

- **Kano model**: Best used when focusing on customer satisfaction and delight. It's particularly useful when trying to identify features that will differentiate the product in the market.

- **WSJF**: Best suited for products where the goal is to maximize economic value by prioritizing features with the highest ROI and minimizing waste.

It's essential to note that these techniques are not mutually exclusive, and multiple approaches can be used in combination to prioritize and estimate user stories effectively.

Introducing WSJF

In Agile development, prioritizing user stories is essential for delivering a valuable product to the end user. WSJF is a prioritization technique that helps teams identify the most valuable work items that need to be done first. This technique is based on a formula that takes into account the cost of delay, job size, and risk reduction. In this chapter, we will explore what WSJF is and how to use it to prioritize user stories.

What is WSJF?

The WSJF prioritization technique is a simple formula that helps teams identify the order in which work items should be done based on their value to the business. It is based on four factors: cost of delay, job size, risk reduction, and opportunity enablement. The formula is as follows:

```
WSJF = (Business Value + Opportunity Enablement + Time Criticality
+ Risk Reduction) / Job Size
```

Business value is the value that the work item will bring to the business, while opportunity enablement is the value that the work item will bring to the end user. Time criticality is the urgency with which the work item needs to be completed, and risk reduction is the degree to which the work item reduces risk.

How to use WSJF to prioritize user stories

To use WSJF to prioritize user stories, you need to follow these steps:

1. Define the value of each user story in terms of business value, opportunity enablement, time criticality, and risk reduction.
2. Estimate the job size of each user story.
3. Calculate the WSJF score for each user story using the formula mentioned previously.
4. Prioritize the user stories based on their WSJF score. Start with the user stories with the highest WSJF score and work your way down the list.

Advantages of WSJF

WSJF provides several advantages for Agile teams, including, for example, the following:

- It helps teams prioritize their work items based on their value to the business and the end user
- It ensures that the most valuable work items are done first, which helps to deliver value to the business and end user as quickly as possible
- It helps to identify and reduce risk by prioritizing work items that reduce risk
- It helps to ensure that the team is working on the right things by prioritizing work items that are time-critical

In summary, the WSJF prioritization technique is a powerful tool that can help Agile teams prioritize their work items and deliver value to the business and end user quickly. By using the WSJF formula to prioritize user stories, teams can ensure that they are working on the most valuable work items and reducing risk in the process.

Suppose a software development team is working on a product to build a new e-commerce website for a client. The team has identified several user stories for the product, including the following:

- As a customer, I want to be able to search for products by name or category
- As a customer, I want to be able to view product details and images
- As a customer, I want to be able to add items to my shopping cart and checkout
- As a customer, I want to be able to create and manage my account
- As a customer service representative, I want to be able to view and manage customer orders
- As an administrator, I want to be able to manage product inventory and pricing

To prioritize these user stories using WSJF, the team would first estimate the time and cost required to implement each story. For simplicity, let's assume that all of the user stories are estimated to take one sprint (two weeks) to implement and cost the same amount.

Next, the team would assess the other factors that contribute to WSJF: user value, time-criticality, and risk reduction. For this product, the team has determined that user value is the most important factor. The team members assign a relative score (between 1 and 10) to each user story based on how much value it would provide to the end user. The scores are as follows:

- Search functionality – 8
- View product details – 7
- Add to cart/checkout – 9
- Account creation/management – 5
- Customer order management – 6
- Product inventory/pricing management – 3

Finally, the team can calculate the WSJF score for each user story by dividing its user value score by its estimated time and cost. The WSJF scores are as follows:

- Search functionality – 4
- View product details – 3.5
- Add to cart/checkout – 4.5
- Account creation/management – 2.5
- Customer order management – 3
- Product inventory/pricing management – 1.5

Based on these scores, the team would prioritize the user stories in the following order:

- Add to cart/checkout
- Search functionality
- View product details
- Customer order management
- Account creation/management
- Product inventory/pricing management

By prioritizing user stories in this way, the team can focus their efforts on delivering the most value to the end user first, while also considering other factors that could impact the success of the product.

The RICE method

Teams must have a clear understanding of which stories are most important to the end user or customer, so they can focus their efforts and resources accordingly. In this section, we will discuss two popular techniques for prioritizing user stories: the RICE method and the Kano model.

RICE is a prioritization framework that was developed by Intercom, a customer messaging platform. It stands for **Reach**, **Impact**, **Confidence**, and **Effort**. The RICE method assigns a numerical score to each of these factors and then combines them to determine a story's overall priority:

- **Reach**: How many people will this story impact? The Reach score takes into account the number of users who will be affected by the feature or improvement.
- **Impact**: How much impact will this story have on users or the business? The Impact score measures the degree of impact that the story will have on users, revenue, or other important business metrics.
- **Confidence**: How confident are we in our ability to deliver this story? The Confidence score reflects the team's level of certainty that they can deliver the feature or improvement within a given timeframe.
- **Effort**: How much effort will it take to deliver this story? The Effort score represents the amount of time, resources, and complexity required to complete the story.

To use the RICE method, each factor is assigned a numerical score between 1 and 10, with 10 being the highest priority. The scores are then multiplied together to produce a total score for each story. Stories with higher scores are given higher priority.

The Kano model

The Kano model is a framework for understanding customer needs and expectations. It was developed by Japanese researcher Noriaki Kano in the 1980s. The Kano model categorizes customer needs into three types – basic needs, performance needs, and delight needs:

- **Basic needs**: These are the essential requirements that must be met for the product to be considered functional. Basic needs are often taken for granted and do not add significant value to the customer's experience.

- **Performance needs**: These are the features that provide incremental value and increase customer satisfaction. Performance needs are often the focus of product development efforts.

- **Delight needs**: These are unexpected or innovative features that provide a "wow" factor and exceed customer expectations. Delight needs can create a strong emotional connection between the customer and the product.

Using the Kano model, user stories are categorized according to the type of need they fulfill. Basic needs are considered necessary but not prioritized, while performance needs are given more attention. Delight needs are the highest priority and can differentiate the product from competitors.

The RICE method and the Kano model are two popular frameworks that can help teams prioritize stories effectively. The RICE method focuses on the potential impact, reach, effort, and confidence of each story, while the Kano model categorizes needs into basic, performance, and delight categories. By using these techniques, teams can focus on the most critical stories and deliver value to customers efficiently.

Approaches for estimating effort – story points and ideal days

When developing software, it is essential to have an accurate estimate of how long it will take to complete a product. Estimating effort is a crucial part of product planning, and user stories are an effective way to break down requirements into manageable chunks. However, estimating the effort required to complete a user story can be a challenge. There are several approaches for estimating effort, including **story points** and **ideal days**.

Story points

Story points are a relative measure of effort that takes into account the complexity, risk, and uncertainty associated with a user story. The development team assigns each story a point value based on its relative size and complexity compared to other stories in the backlog. Story points are not based on time, but rather on the team's collective experience and understanding of the work required to complete a story.

The most common way to assign story points is by using the Fibonacci sequence, with each number representing a relative size and complexity of the story. For example, a simple story might be given a point value of 1, while a more complex story might be given a point value of 5, 8, 13, or even higher.

Ideal days

Ideal days is a more traditional approach for estimating effort. It involves estimating the number of ideal working days required to complete a user story. Ideal days takes into account factors such as team velocity, available resources, and any external dependencies that may impact the completion of the story.

The team estimates how many ideal working days it would take to complete a story, assuming no distractions or interruptions. Ideal days is usually a more accurate measure of time than story points, but it can be more time-consuming to estimate.

Which approach to choose

The choice of approach depends on the team's preferences and the context of the product. Story points is a more flexible approach, allowing the team to account for the complexity and uncertainty of a product. Ideal days, on the other hand, provides a more accurate estimate of the time required, but it may not be as adaptable to changing circumstances.

In general, story points is a better fit for Agile methodologies, which prioritize flexibility and responsiveness over strict adherence to a plan. Ideal days is better suited for products with a fixed timeline, where the emphasis is on completing the work within a specified timeframe.

Estimating effort is a vital part of product planning, and there are several approaches available, including story points and ideal days. The choice of approach depends on the context of the product and the preferences of the development team. Regardless of the approach chosen, it is essential to regularly review and adjust estimates based on actual progress and changing circumstances.

Factors to consider when estimating user stories

Estimating the effort required to complete user stories is an essential aspect of Agile software development. The accuracy of estimates has a significant impact on product planning and progress tracking. However, estimating accurately can be challenging, as it requires considering several factors that may impact the effort required to complete a user story. In this section, we will discuss some of the factors to consider when estimating user stories.

Complexity

The complexity of a user story is another important factor to consider when estimating effort. The complexity of a user story is determined by the number of tasks required to complete it, as well as any technical challenges that may arise.

When estimating the complexity of a user story, it's essential to consider the skills and experience of the team members who will be working on it. A complex story may require more experienced team members, which can impact the overall effort required to complete the story.

Dependencies

Dependencies can impact the effort required to complete a user story. Dependencies occur when one story cannot be completed until another story is finished. For example, if a user story requires a database migration, the migration must be completed before the user story can be finished.

Dependencies can impact the team's velocity, as they may cause delays in completing user stories. When estimating effort, it's essential to consider any dependencies that may impact the team's ability to complete the user story.

Risks

Uncertainty is a factor that can impact the accuracy of estimates. There may be uncertainty around the requirements of a user story, which can impact the effort required to complete it. Additionally, technical challenges may arise during development, which can impact the effort required to complete a user story.

When estimating effort, it's essential to consider uncertainty and build in some contingency time. This will help to account for any unexpected challenges that may arise during development.

Estimating the effort required to complete user stories is an important aspect of Agile software development. When estimating, it's essential to consider factors such as team velocity, complexity, dependencies, and uncertainty. By considering these factors, you can improve the accuracy of your estimates and make better-informed decisions when planning and tracking your product.

Cycle time, lead time, and throughput introduction

When working on software development products, it's essential to have a good understanding of the different factors that can impact the time it takes to complete a user story. Estimating the effort required for a story is a critical aspect of Agile development, as it helps the team to prioritize tasks and ensure that the product remains on track. In this section, we will discuss some of the key factors that should be taken into account when estimating user stories, including cycle time, lead time, and throughput.

Cycle time

Cycle time is the time it takes for a team to complete a user story from start to finish. It's important to measure cycle time accurately as it can help to identify bottlenecks or areas of the development process that can be improved. One way to improve cycle time is by breaking down stories into smaller, more manageable tasks that can be completed more quickly.

Lead time

Lead time is the time it takes for a team to complete a user story from the moment it is added to the backlog to the moment it is marked as complete. Lead time can be impacted by a range of factors, including the complexity of the story, the team's skill level, and any dependencies on other stories. By tracking the lead time, the team can identify any patterns or issues that are causing delays in the development process.

Throughput

Throughput is the number of user stories that a team completes in a given period. It's important to measure throughput as it can help the team to estimate how long it will take to complete a specific number of stories. This is particularly useful when planning sprints, as it helps to ensure that the team is not taking on more work than they can realistically complete.

In conclusion, understanding the factors that impact the time and effort required to complete user stories is essential for effective Agile development. By considering cycle time, lead time, and throughput, as well as other factors, such as complexity, dependencies, and uncertainty, the team can make more accurate estimates and prioritize tasks more effectively. By continually monitoring and analyzing these factors, the team can identify areas for improvement and optimize the development process.

Best practices for prioritization and estimation in Agile development products

Effective prioritization ensures that the development team works on the most valuable features first, while estimation helps in planning and managing product timelines. In this section, we will discuss best practices for prioritization and estimation in Agile development products:

- **Involve stakeholders**: It is important to involve stakeholders, such as product owners and users, in the prioritization process to ensure that their needs and requirements are considered. Their feedback and insights can help in identifying the most valuable user stories.

- **Use a structured approach**: Using a structured approach, such as MoSCoW or Value-based prioritization, can help in prioritizing user stories based on their importance and value. This ensures that the most valuable stories are worked on first.

- **Estimate using relative sizing**: Relative sizing, such as story points or ideal days, can be more effective than estimating in hours as it avoids the pitfall of committing to fixed timelines. It allows for more flexibility in product planning and helps in managing stakeholder expectations.

- **Account for complexity**: The complexity of user stories should be considered when estimating effort. More complex stories may require more effort and resources than simpler ones.

- **Track cycle time, lead time, and throughput**: Measuring cycle time, lead time, and throughput can help in improving the accuracy of estimation by providing historical data on how long it takes for user stories to move through the development process.

- **Revisit and refine**: Priorities and estimations should be revisited and refined regularly to ensure that they remain relevant and accurate as the product progresses. Regularly reviewing priorities and estimations can help in identifying potential risks and roadblocks.

By involving stakeholders, using structured approaches, estimating using relative sizing, considering team velocity and complexity, and tracking cycle time, lead time, and throughput, development teams can ensure that they are working on the most valuable stories and that product timelines are realistic. Regularly revisiting and refining priorities and estimations can help in identifying potential risks and roadblocks and ensure that the product stays on track.

#NoEstimates introduction

In Agile software development, estimating the time and effort required for user stories is an important aspect of planning and delivering successful products. However, in recent years, a movement called **#NoEstimates** has gained popularity, advocating for a different approach to product planning and delivery. In this section, we will explore the #NoEstimates movement and its key principles, as well as examine the advantages and disadvantages of this approach.

The traditional approach to software development often involves extensive estimation efforts to predict product timelines and budgets. However, the Agile movement has challenged this practice and introduced the concept of #NoEstimates. #NoEstimates advocates argue that estimation can be time-consuming, inaccurate, and counterproductive to the iterative and adaptive nature of Agile development.

In this chapter, we will delve into the #NoEstimates movement and explore its principles and practices. We will examine the arguments for and against estimation in Agile products and discuss alternative approaches that focus on value delivery, continuous improvement, and collaboration. By understanding the #NoEstimates mindset and exploring different perspectives, you will gain insights into how to navigate the estimation dilemma and make informed decisions about estimating or not estimating in your own products.

Through real-world examples and case studies, we will illustrate the practical application of #NoEstimates principles and demonstrate the potential benefits and challenges of adopting this approach. By the end of this section, you will have a deeper understanding of the #NoEstimates movement and be equipped with valuable insights to guide your decision-making process regarding estimation practices in Agile development.

What is the #NoEstimates movement?

The #NoEstimates movement is a philosophy that encourages teams to focus on delivering value rather than spending time on estimates. The movement challenges the traditional approach to software development that places a heavy emphasis on estimating the time and cost of products before development even begins.

Instead of spending significant time on estimates, #NoEstimates proponents argue that Agile teams should focus on delivering small, iterative increments of value to customers. By focusing on delivering value incrementally, teams can receive constant feedback from stakeholders and adjust their work accordingly. Exploring the limitations of traditional estimation practices and embracing a more flexible approach, there are alternative methods and principles that can guide decision-making in Agile products. These include understanding the no estimates movement, prioritizing value-based decision making, relying on empirical data, and fostering a culture of continuous feedback:

1. **Exploring the limitations of traditional estimation practices**: Traditional estimation techniques, such as bottom-up and top-down approaches, often struggle to provide accurate estimates in Agile products. The inherent complexity and uncertainty make it challenging to accurately predict effort and timeframes. This section examines the limitations of traditional estimation practices in the context of Agile development and the impact they can have on product success.

2. **Understanding the #NoEstimates movement**: The #NoEstimates movement is a response to the challenges and limitations of traditional estimation practices. It advocates for a shift in mindset and a departure from the reliance on estimation in favor of value-based decision-making, empirical data, and continuous feedback loops. The following sublist explores the principles and motivations behind the #NoEstimates movement, shedding light on the rationale for seeking alternative approaches to estimation in Agile development:

    I.   **Value-based decision-making**: One of the core principles of the #NoEstimates movement is the emphasis on value-based decision-making. Instead of focusing solely on estimation, the focus shifts to understanding and prioritizing value delivery. This point delves into the concept of value-based decision-making, exploring techniques such as impact mapping, hypothesis-driven development, and value-driven prioritization.

    II. **Empirical data and continuous feedback**: Another key aspect of the #NoEstimates movement is the reliance on empirical data and continuous feedback loops. By leveraging real-time data and feedback from stakeholders and users, teams can make informed decisions and adapt their plans accordingly. This point explores the importance of continuous feedback and data-driven decision-making in the context of Agile development, highlighting techniques for gathering and utilizing data effectively.

Advantages of #NoEstimates

One of the key advantages of the #NoEstimates movement is that it allows teams to focus on delivering value rather than spending time on estimates. By working in small increments, teams can quickly iterate and adjust their work based on feedback from stakeholders.

Another advantage is that by not focusing on estimates, teams can avoid the pressure to commit to specific deadlines and delivery dates. This can help to reduce stress and improve team morale, leading to a more productive and enjoyable work environment.

Disadvantages of #NoEstimates

One of the main criticisms of the #NoEstimates movement is that it can be difficult to plan and manage large-scale products without estimates. Without estimates, it can be challenging to determine the appropriate resources and staffing needed for a product, which can lead to delays and budget overruns.

Another disadvantage is that without estimates, it can be difficult to communicate product progress and timelines to stakeholders. This can lead to misunderstandings and dissatisfaction among stakeholders, which can ultimately impact the success of the product.

The #NoEstimates movement is a growing philosophy in the Agile software development community, emphasizing a focus on delivering value rather than spending time on estimates. While this approach has its advantages, it may not be suitable for all types of projects or teams. Ultimately, the decision to use estimates or not will depend on the specific needs and requirements of the product, as well as the preferences and capabilities of the development team.

Concrete examples of prioritizing and estimating user stories

When conducting prioritization and estimation exercises in Agile development, it is crucial to involve a diverse group of individuals who can provide different perspectives and insights. The following are the types of people who should be present for these exercises:

- **Product Owner**: The Product Owner represents the voice of the customer and is responsible for defining and prioritizing the product backlog. Their involvement is crucial as they provide insights into customer needs, market trends, and business priorities.

- **Development team**: The development team consists of individuals responsible for delivering the product. Their expertise and understanding of technical feasibility are essential when estimating the effort required for user stories. They contribute valuable insights during prioritization discussions and provide input on dependencies and implementation considerations.

- **Scrum Master**: The Scrum Master facilitates the prioritization and estimation exercises, ensuring that the process is collaborative, efficient, and focused. They help the team understand the purpose of the exercises and guide discussions to reach a consensus.

- **Stakeholders**: Stakeholders, including business representatives, subject matter experts, and other relevant parties, should be involved in the prioritization and estimation process. Their perspectives help ensure that the product aligns with organizational goals and customer expectations.

- **UX/UI designers**: Involving UX/UI designers during prioritization and estimation exercises is valuable as they provide insights into the user experience and interface design. Their expertise helps in understanding the impact of user stories on usability and overall product quality.

- **Domain experts**: Depending on the nature of the product, domain experts with specialized knowledge or subject matter expertise may be required. Their insights contribute to more accurate estimations and informed prioritization decisions.

It is important to note that the specific individuals involved may vary based on the product and organizational context. The key is to have a cross-functional and collaborative team that represents the necessary expertise and perspectives to make informed decisions during prioritization and estimation exercises.

In the previous sections, we discussed the importance of prioritizing and estimating user stories in Agile development. Now, let's take a look at some concrete examples of how to apply these concepts in practice.

Example 1 – online retail store

Let's say we are working on an online retail store product. Here are some sample user stories we need to prioritize and estimate:

- As a customer, I want to be able to filter products by brand so that I can easily find the products I'm interested in

- As a customer, I want to be able to view my order history so that I can track my purchases

- As a customer, I want to be able to leave a review for a product so that I can share my feedback with other customers

- As a store owner, I want to be able to track inventory levels so that I can replenish stock when necessary

To prioritize these user stories, we can use the MoSCoW method, where we categorize them as Must Haves, Should Haves, Could Haves, or Won't Haves. For example, filtering products by brand may be a Must Have for the online retail store, while leaving a review for a product may be a Could Have.

For estimating, we can use story points. The team can assign a point value to each story based on its complexity and the effort required to implement it. For example, the story to track inventory levels may be more complex and require more effort than the story to view order history.

Example 2 – social media platform

Let's say we are working on a social media platform product. Here are some sample user stories we need to prioritize and estimate:

- As a user, I want to be able to share posts with my friends so that I can keep them up to date on my life

- As a user, I want to be able to search for other users so that I can connect with them

- As a user, I want to be able to set my privacy settings so that I can control who sees my posts

- As an administrator, I want to be able to monitor user activity so that I can ensure the platform is being used appropriately

To prioritize these user stories, we can use Value-based prioritization. We can assign a value to each story based on its potential impact on the users and the business. For example, the story to search for other users may have a higher value because it could increase user engagement on the platform.

For estimating, we can use ideal days. The team can estimate the number of ideal days required to implement each story. For example, the story to monitor user activity may require more ideal days than the story to share posts with friends.

Prioritizing and estimating user stories are crucial activities in Agile development products. By using techniques such as MoSCoW, Value-based prioritization, story points, and ideal days, teams can effectively prioritize and estimate user stories. The examples we discussed show how these techniques can be applied in practice. It is important to keep in mind that each product and team is unique, so it's essential to tailor these techniques to the product's specific needs.

Summary

In this chapter, we explored the importance of prioritizing and estimating user stories in Agile development products. We discussed techniques for prioritizing user stories, including MoSCoW and Value-based prioritization. We also covered approaches for estimating effort, including story points and ideal days, and discussed factors to consider when estimating, such as team velocity, complexity, cycle time, lead time, and throughput.

Additionally, we discussed best practices for effective prioritization and estimation in Agile development products, such as involving the whole team, breaking down stories into smaller, more manageable pieces, and using data to inform estimates.

Lastly, we delved into the #NoEstimates movement, which advocates moving away from traditional estimation methods in favor of more iterative and data-driven approaches.

Overall, prioritizing and estimating user stories is critical to the success of Agile development products, and teams must carefully consider their options and best practices to ensure accurate estimates and effective prioritization. In the next chapter, *Chapter 5, Working with Stakeholders*, we will explore strategies for effectively collaborating with stakeholders throughout the Agile development process to ensure the success of the product.

Questions

1. What do we do if our team is struggling to come up with estimates for a particular user story?
2. How do we handle changing priorities mid-sprint?
3. What happens if our estimates turn out to be wrong?
4. What's the difference between MoSCoW and Value-based prioritization?

Answers

1. It's important to remember that estimates are just that – estimates. They are not guarantees or promises. If a team is struggling to come up with an estimate for a story, they may want to break it down further into smaller, more manageable pieces. Alternatively, they could try using relative estimation techniques, such as story points or T-shirt sizing. It's also important to remember that some stories may inherently be more difficult to estimate than others, and that's okay.

2. Changing priorities mid-sprint can be challenging, but it's a reality of Agile development. If a high-priority story emerges during a sprint, the team should evaluate whether it's possible to add it to the sprint or whether it needs to wait until the next one. If a lower-priority story becomes less important or unnecessary, the team may need to reevaluate its priority and potentially remove it from the sprint backlog. In either case, communication and collaboration are key.

3. Estimates are just that – estimates. They are not guarantees or promises. It's important to treat estimates as a tool for planning and decision-making rather than a set-in-stone commitment. If the team's estimates turn out to be off, they should reflect on what went wrong and adjust their estimation process accordingly. Additionally, they should use the data from previous sprints to inform future estimates and continually refine their estimation process.

4. MoSCoW and Value-based prioritization are both techniques for prioritizing user stories, but they have different approaches. MoSCoW stands for Must Have, Should Have, Could Have, and Won't Have. With MoSCoW, stories are classified into these categories based on their relative importance. Value-based prioritization, on the other hand, involves assigning a numerical value to each story based on its potential value to the user or the business. Ultimately, both techniques can be effective, and the choice between them may depend on the specific needs of the team and product.

5
Working with Stakeholders

In this chapter, we will focus on working with stakeholders in Agile products. Stakeholders are individuals or groups who have an interest in the product and its outcome. These are product owners, users, the dev team, management, legal, security, and support. They can be internal or external to the organization and have different needs and expectations. Stakeholder engagement is essential for the success of Agile products, and effective communication is key to building trust and maintaining a positive relationship with stakeholders.

In this chapter, we will discuss how to work with stakeholders to ensure their needs are met and how to keep them engaged throughout the project. In the Agile methodology, stakeholders are individuals or groups who have a vested interest in the success of the product. They can be internal or external to the organization, and their involvement is critical for product success. Working effectively with stakeholders requires open communication, transparency, and collaboration. We will explore the best practices for working with stakeholders in an Agile product.

In this chapter, we're going to cover the following main topics:

- Gathering requirements and building a product backlog
- Communicating user stories to a different team
- Identifying and categorizing stakeholders
- Defining stakeholder roles and responsibilities
- Managing stakeholder expectations
- Communicating effectively with stakeholders
- Keeping stakeholders engaged throughout the product

By the end of this chapter, readers will be able to effectively identify, categorize, and engage stakeholders in Agile products. They will understand how to manage stakeholder expectations, define roles and responsibilities, and communicate effectively to keep stakeholders engaged throughout the project. The knowledge gained from this chapter will help readers ensure the success of their Agile products by building strong relationships with stakeholders and ensuring their needs are met.

Building a product backlog

Gathering requirements and building a product backlog is a critical step in Agile development that lays the foundation for the entire product. In this section, we will explore the best practices for gathering requirements, building a product backlog, and prioritizing items based on stakeholder needs. By the end of this section, readers will be able to create a comprehensive product backlog that accurately reflects stakeholder needs and is prioritized for efficient development.

We're going to cover the following main topics:

- **Understanding the importance of requirements gathering**: In this section, we'll discuss why requirements gathering is important and how it can help to ensure that the product meets stakeholder needs
- **Techniques for gathering requirements**: We'll explore some key techniques for gathering requirements, including stakeholder interviews, surveys, and user testing
- **Creating a product backlog**: We'll discuss how to create a product backlog that accurately reflects stakeholders' needs and is organized for efficient development
- **Prioritizing items in the backlog**: We'll explore different techniques for prioritizing items in the backlog, including MoSCoW and value-based prioritization
- **Refining the product backlog**: We'll discuss how to continuously refine the product backlog based on stakeholder feedback and changing product requirements

Understanding the importance of requirements gathering

Requirements gathering is a critical step in Agile development as it lays the foundation for the entire product. Effective requirements gathering ensures that the development team has a clear understanding of stakeholder needs and can develop a product that meets those needs. It also helps to identify potential issues early in the development process, saving time and resources in the long run.

Techniques for gathering requirements

There are several techniques for gathering requirements in Agile development, including stakeholder interviews, surveys, and user testing. Stakeholder interviews involve speaking directly with stakeholders to understand their needs and requirements for the product. Surveys can be used to gather feedback from a larger group of stakeholders, while user testing involves observing how users interact with a product to identify potential issues.

Creating a product backlog

The product backlog is a comprehensive list of features, enhancements, and bug fixes that need to be developed for the product. The product owner is responsible for creating and maintaining the product backlog, ensuring that it accurately reflects stakeholder needs and is organized for efficient development.

Prioritizing items in the backlog

Prioritizing items in the product backlog is essential to ensure that the development team is working on the most important items first. MoSCoW and value-based prioritization are two techniques that can be used to prioritize items based on stakeholder needs and the value they bring to the product.

Refining the product backlog

The product backlog is a living document that should be continuously refined based on stakeholder feedback and changing product requirements. Regularly reviewing and refining the product backlog ensures that the development team is working on the most important items and that the product continues to meet stakeholder needs.

Gathering requirements and building a product backlog is a critical step in Agile development that ensures that the development team has a clear understanding of stakeholder needs and can develop a product that meets those needs. By using the techniques and best practices discussed in this chapter, readers can create a comprehensive product backlog that accurately reflects stakeholder needs and is organized for efficient development.

Communicating user stories effectively

User stories are an essential component of Agile development and ensure that the end product meets the user's needs. However, communicating these user stories effectively to the development team is equally important to ensure that everyone is on the same page. In this section, we will discuss some tips and techniques for communicating user stories effectively to different teams involved in the development process:

- **Understanding different team members and their roles**: In Agile development, there are different team members involved, including developers, testers, designers, product owners, and more. We'll discuss the roles and responsibilities of each team member and how they contribute to the development process.

- **Creating a shared understanding of user stories**: User stories need to be communicated clearly to the development team so that everyone has a shared understanding of the requirements. We'll discuss techniques such as creating wireframes, mockups, and visual aids to help communicate user stories effectively.

- **Breaking down complex user stories**: Sometimes, user stories can be complex and difficult to understand. We'll explore techniques such as breaking down user stories into smaller, more manageable pieces and creating prototypes to help communicate complex user stories effectively.

- **Effective collaboration and communication**: Collaboration and communication are key to ensuring that user stories are communicated effectively to the development team. We'll discuss techniques such as daily stand-up meetings, sprint retrospectives, and using Agile tools to help teams collaborate effectively.

- **Tailoring communication to different team members**: Different team members have different communication styles and preferences. We'll discuss techniques for tailoring communication to different team members, such as using visual aids for designers, providing detailed technical specifications for developers, and more.

Stakeholder identification

The first step in working with stakeholders is to identify who they are. Stakeholders include customers, end users, product sponsors, subject-matter experts, and other interested parties. It's essential to identify all stakeholders early in the project to ensure that their needs and expectations are understood and incorporated into the product plan.

In any product, it is essential to identify and categorize stakeholders as they can impact and influence the product's success. They can be internal or external to the organization and can have varying levels of involvement and influence.

In this section, we will cover the following main topics:

- The importance of identifying and categorizing stakeholders
- Types of stakeholders
- Techniques for identifying stakeholders
- Categorizing stakeholders based on their level of involvement and influence

Identifying key stakeholders

The first step in keeping stakeholders engaged is to identify who they are. Key stakeholders include product sponsors, customers, end users, team members, and any other groups or individuals who have a vested interest in the product. Identifying stakeholders and their needs is critical to developing an effective communication plan.

The importance of identifying and categorizing stakeholders

Identifying and categorizing stakeholders is crucial as it helps in understanding who is involved and who can impact the product's outcome. It enables us to determine how much effort and resources should be allocated to engaging and communicating with stakeholders. By identifying and categorizing stakeholders, we can prioritize their needs and expectations and manage potential conflicts and risks.

Types of stakeholders

There are various types of stakeholders, including internal and external stakeholders. Internal stakeholders can be employees, managers, executives, or shareholders. External stakeholders can be customers, suppliers, partners, government entities, or regulatory bodies. It is important to consider all types of stakeholders as they can impact the product's success differently. Here's an overview of the key stakeholders in a project or product development and their roles:

- **Product owner**: The product owner is responsible for defining the vision, prioritizing features, and making decisions regarding the product. They act as the voice of the customer and ensure that the product meets the user's needs and business goals.

- **Users**: Users are the individuals who will use the product or benefit from its features. Their feedback and insights are crucial ways to understand their needs, preferences, and pain points. User involvement helps shape the product to ensure it delivers value and meets user expectations.

- **Development team**: The development team consists of individuals responsible for building and delivering the product. They are involved in the technical implementation and work closely with the product owner to understand the requirements and translate them into working solutions.

- **Management**: Management stakeholders provide overall guidance, support, and resources for the product. They make high-level decisions, provide strategic direction, and ensure that the product aligns with organizational objectives. Management stakeholders play a crucial role in setting priorities and allocating resources.

- **Data analysts**: Data analysts play a vital role in analyzing and interpreting data related to the product or project. They provide insights and recommendations based on data analysis, helping the team make data-driven decisions and measure the success of the product.

- **Legal**: Legal stakeholders ensure that the product complies with applicable laws, regulations, and industry standards. They assess legal risks, review contracts, and provide guidance on intellectual property, privacy, and compliance matters.

- **Security**: Security stakeholders focus on ensuring the product's security and protecting sensitive information. They assess and mitigate security risks, implement security measures, and help define security requirements for the product.

- **Sales**: Sales stakeholders provide valuable market insights and customer feedback. They play a role in understanding market trends, identifying customer needs and preferences, and helping to shape the product's features and positioning.

- **Support**: Support stakeholders handle customer inquiries, feedback, and issue resolution. They provide insights into common user problems and suggestions for product improvements. Their feedback helps shape the product's ongoing support and maintenance strategy.

- **Operations/manufacturing**: Operations or manufacturing stakeholders are involved when the product involves physical production, assembly, or distribution. They provide input on production processes and supply chain logistics and ensure smooth operations once the product is launched.

These stakeholders represent the range of expertise and perspectives needed for a successful project or product development. Effective collaboration is crucial for gathering requirements, making informed decisions, and ensuring that the final product meets the needs and expectations of all parties involved.

Techniques for identifying stakeholders

There are several techniques (data from past engagements is also a good starting point) for identifying stakeholders, including brainstorming sessions, interviews, focus groups, surveys, and stakeholder mapping:

- **Brainstorming sessions** involve bringing together a diverse group of individuals to generate a list of potential stakeholders

- **Interviews**, and **surveys** involve engaging with stakeholders directly to gather their needs and expectations

- **Stakeholder mapping** involves visualizing the stakeholder landscape and relationships to identify key stakeholders

Categorizing stakeholders based on their level of involvement and influence

Stakeholders can be categorized based on their level of involvement and influence. The categorization can be done using a power/interest matrix or a salience model. The power/interest matrix categorizes stakeholders based on their level of power and interest in the product. The salience model categorizes stakeholders based on their level of power, urgency, and legitimacy. By categorizing stakeholders, we can determine the appropriate level of engagement and communication needed for each stakeholder group.

In conclusion, identifying and categorizing stakeholders is crucial for the success of any project. By understanding their needs and expectations, we can prioritize our efforts and resources to engage and communicate with them effectively. By using the techniques and models mentioned in this section, we can categorize stakeholders based on their level of involvement and influence and manage potential conflicts and risks.

Managing stakeholder expectations

Managing stakeholder expectations is critical for product success. It's important to ensure that stakeholders have a clear understanding of the product's objectives, scope, timeline, and budget. Regular communication is essential to keeping stakeholders informed of the product's progress and any changes to the plan.

Stakeholder management is a crucial aspect of product management, and managing stakeholder expectations is essential for a product to be successful. Managing stakeholder expectations involves understanding stakeholders' needs, managing communication with them, and ensuring that their expectations are aligned with product goals. In this section, we will discuss strategies for managing stakeholder expectations and maintaining positive relationships with stakeholders.

We will cover the following main topics:

- Understanding stakeholder expectations
- Communication management
- Setting and managing expectations
- Handling stakeholder resistance

Understanding stakeholder expectations

The first step in managing stakeholder expectations is to understand their needs and expectations. Stakeholders may have different needs, goals, and expectations, and it's essential to identify and categorize them based on their level of interest and influence. Once stakeholders are identified and categorized, you can create a stakeholder management plan that outlines how you will engage with them and manage their expectations throughout the project.

Communication management

Effective communication is key to managing stakeholder expectations. You should have a communication plan that outlines how you will communicate with stakeholders, including the frequency, mode of communication, and message content. You should also consider the language and tone used in your communication and ensure that it's tailored to the stakeholders' needs and preferences.

Setting and managing expectations

It's important to set realistic expectations with stakeholders and ensure that they align with the product goals. This involves managing stakeholder requirements, scope, timelines, and budget. You should also communicate any changes or issues that may affect the product's progress or outcomes promptly.

Keeping stakeholders engaged

Keeping stakeholders engaged throughout the project is essential to ensuring that the project runs smoothly and meets the needs and expectations of all parties involved. In this section, we will explore strategies for keeping stakeholders engaged and informed throughout the product life cycle.

The importance of stakeholder engagement

Stakeholder engagement is crucial to a product's success. Engaged stakeholders provide input, feedback, and support, which can help ensure that the product meets its goals and objectives. Engaging stakeholders also helps to build trust, foster collaboration, and minimize resistance to change.

Handling stakeholder resistance

Stakeholders may resist changes or decisions that affect their interests or expectations. You should be prepared to handle resistance by understanding the stakeholders' concerns, addressing them, and offering alternatives or solutions that meet their needs and align with the product goals. You should also consider the impact of stakeholder resistance on the product and develop a contingency plan to mitigate it.

In conclusion, managing stakeholder expectations is essential for product success. By understanding stakeholder needs, managing communication, setting realistic expectations, and handling resistance, you can maintain positive relationships with stakeholders and ensure that product outcomes meet their needs and expectations.

Collaboration

Collaboration is one of the essential principles of the Agile methodology. In Agile, collaboration refers to working closely with stakeholders, team members, and customers to achieve the product goals effectively. Collaboration is essential to ensuring that everyone is on the same page, that all requirements are understood, and that the product progresses as smoothly as possible.

In Agile products, stakeholders are active participants throughout the product's life cycle. Collaboration comprises regular communication, including stand-up meetings, demos, retrospectives, and joint decision-making. By involving stakeholders throughout the product, you can ensure that their input is incorporated into the final product.

In this section, we will discuss the importance of collaboration in the Agile methodology and explore some strategies for successful collaboration. We're going to cover the following main topics:

- Understanding the importance of collaboration in the Agile methodology
- Strategies for successful collaboration
- Communication and collaboration tools

Understanding the importance of collaboration in the Agile methodology

Collaboration plays a vital role in the Agile methodology. The Agile process is designed to promote collaboration between stakeholders, team members, and customers to ensure that everyone is working toward a common goal. Collaboration helps in understanding the product requirements, identifying risks, and mitigating potential issues.

Collaboration allows the team to have a better understanding of the product and helps in the development of a shared vision. This shared vision ensures that everyone is working toward the same objective and helps in minimizing any ambiguity or misunderstandings.

Strategies for successful collaboration

Successful collaboration requires effort from all parties involved. The following strategies can help to ensure effective collaboration:

- **Establishing clear goals**: Clearly defining the product goals and objectives is critical to ensure that everyone is working toward a common goal. This helps in minimizing any confusion or misunderstandings.

- **Open and frequent communication**: Communication is the key to successful collaboration. Regular communication between stakeholders, team members, and customers helps in identifying risks and potential issues, and ensuring everyone is on the same page.

- **Building trust**: Building trust between stakeholders and team members is crucial for effective collaboration. Trust ensures that everyone is working together toward a common goal and fosters an environment of open communication and transparency.

- **Embracing diversity**: Diversity is an essential aspect of collaboration. By embracing diverse viewpoints and experiences, the team can identify potential issues and develop innovative solutions to overcome them.

Communication and collaboration tools

The Agile methodology provides several communication and collaboration tools to ensure effective collaboration. These tools include daily stand-up meetings, sprint planning sessions, sprint reviews, and retrospectives:

- **Daily stand-up meetings**: Also known as a "daily scrum," this is a daily meeting where team members gather to discuss progress, identify any blockers or issues, and plan their work for the day. Each team member answers three questions: What did I accomplish yesterday? What am I planning to do today? Are there any obstacles in my way?

- **Sprint planning sessions**: This is a meeting where the team comes together to plan the work that will be completed in the upcoming sprint. The team reviews the product backlog, discusses the priorities, and decides which items will be included in the sprint backlog. The team estimates the effort required for each item and creates a plan for completing the work.

- **Sprint reviews**: At the end of each sprint, the team holds a sprint review to demonstrate the work completed during the sprint. This is an opportunity for the team to receive feedback from stakeholders and customers and discuss any changes or updates that need to be made.

- **Retrospectives**: After each sprint, the team holds a retrospective to review the previous sprint and identify ways to improve for the next one. The team discusses what went well, what didn't go well, and what changes can be made to improve processes, communication, and teamwork.

These tools are designed to improve communication, collaboration, and productivity among team members and ensure that everyone is working toward the same goals. By using these tools effectively, teams can ensure that user stories are communicated clearly and that everyone is on the same page.

Additionally, there are several communication tools such as email, instant messaging, video conferencing, and collaborative software that can help the team collaborate effectively.

Developing a communication plan

A communication plan outlines how information will be shared with stakeholders throughout the project. The plan should include the types of information to be shared, the frequency of communication, and the methods used to communicate. Communication should be two-way and should involve active listening and feedback from stakeholders.

Regular check-ins

Regular check-ins with stakeholders can help keep them engaged and informed. These check-ins can be in the form of meetings, emails, or other forms of communication. They provide an opportunity for stakeholders to ask questions, provide feedback, and get updates on the product's progress.

Providing transparency

Transparency is critical to keeping stakeholders engaged. It involves providing stakeholders with access to relevant information, such as product plans, timelines, budgets, and risks. Transparency helps build trust and enables stakeholders to understand the product's progress and potential impact on their business or organization.

Addressing concerns

Finally, it is important to address any concerns or issues that stakeholders may have throughout the project. This involves active listening, empathy, and a willingness to find solutions that meet stakeholders' needs. By addressing concerns promptly, stakeholders will feel heard and valued, which can help keep them engaged and supportive throughout the project.

Keeping stakeholders engaged throughout the project is essential to ensuring its success. By identifying key stakeholders, developing a communication plan, providing transparency, and addressing concerns, product teams can foster collaboration and build trust with stakeholders.

Prioritization in Agile products

Prioritization is critical. Stakeholders play a significant role in prioritizing user stories and defining the product's scope. It's important to work closely with stakeholders to ensure that user stories are prioritized based on their value to the customer and the product's objectives.

Conflict resolution

Working with stakeholders can sometimes lead to conflict. It's essential to have a conflict resolution plan in place to manage any issues that arise. The Agile coach can play a critical role in facilitating conflict resolution and ensuring that all parties feel heard and that a mutually acceptable solution is reached.

In an Agile product, conflicts can arise from various sources, including differences in opinions, misunderstandings, competing priorities, and communication breakdowns. As a stakeholder in an Agile product, you may encounter conflicts that require resolution. In this section, we'll discuss some effective conflict resolution techniques that you can use to resolve conflicts and ensure a positive outcome for the product.

Understanding the conflict

The first step in resolving any conflict is to understand it. You need to identify the source of the conflict, the parties involved, and the impact it may have on the product. Talk to the stakeholders involved, listen to their perspectives, and gather as much information as possible before deciding on a course of action. Understanding the conflict will help you determine the best approach to resolving it.

Collaboration and compromise

Collaboration and compromise are two effective techniques for resolving conflicts. Collaboration involves working together with the stakeholders involved to find a mutually beneficial solution. In a collaborative approach, all stakeholders are involved in the decision-making process, and the focus is on finding a solution that satisfies everyone. Compromise, on the other hand, involves finding a middle ground that is acceptable to all parties involved. In this approach, each stakeholder gives up something to achieve a mutually acceptable outcome.

Active listening

Active listening is an essential skill for conflict resolution. To resolve a conflict, you need to understand the perspectives and needs of all parties involved. Active listening involves paying attention to what the stakeholders are saying, asking clarifying questions, and acknowledging their concerns. It's important to show empathy and respect for the stakeholders' perspectives, even if you don't agree with them.

Negotiation

Negotiation involves finding a compromise that is acceptable to all parties involved. In negotiation, you need to identify the stakeholders' needs, understand their positions, and find a solution that meets everyone's needs. Effective negotiation requires good communication skills, the ability to identify common ground, and the willingness to explore creative solutions.

Escalation

Sometimes, conflicts cannot be resolved through collaboration, compromise, active listening, or negotiation. In these cases, it may be necessary to escalate the conflict to a higher authority or an external mediator. Escalation should be a last resort, and you should only do so if you have exhausted all other options. When escalating a conflict, you should provide a clear explanation of the issue, the steps you have taken to try and resolve it, and the impact it may have on the product.

Conflict resolution is an essential skill for stakeholders in Agile products. By understanding the conflict, collaborating, compromising, practicing active listening, negotiating effectively, and knowing when to escalate, you can resolve conflicts and ensure a positive outcome for the product. Remember that conflicts are a natural part of any course of product development and resolving them effectively is key to product success.

Crucial conversations

Effective communication is essential in any Agile development product. However, when stakeholders have different expectations, opinions, or interests, this can lead to conflict and misunderstandings. In such situations, having the skills to hold crucial conversations becomes critical for product success.

According to *Crucial Conversations*, by Joseph Grenny, Kerry Patterson, Al Switzler, and Ron McMillan, a crucial conversation is a discussion between two or more people where opinions differ, stakes are high, and emotions run strong. Handling such conversations poorly can have serious consequences for the product, including delays, low team morale, and a suboptimal product.

In this section, we'll discuss crucial conversations, their importance in Agile development, and some key techniques for holding successful conversations.

We'll cover the following topics:

- **Understanding what constitutes a crucial conversation**: We'll explore what constitutes a crucial conversation and how it differs from a regular conversation
- **The importance of crucial conversations in Agile development**: We'll discuss why crucial conversations are essential in Agile development products and how they can impact product outcomes
- **Techniques for holding crucial conversations**: We'll discuss some key techniques for holding crucial conversations, including creating a safe environment, using active listening, and making your point of view clear
- **Steps for preparing for a crucial conversation**: We'll explore some important steps you should take to prepare for a crucial conversation, including understanding your own emotions and goals and identifying the other party's perspectives and interests
- **Examples of crucial conversations in Agile development**: We'll provide some examples of crucial conversations that might arise in an Agile development product, and how to handle them effectively

Understanding what constitutes a crucial conversation

These conversations are often challenging and uncomfortable and require a high level of emotional intelligence to navigate successfully. They are not the same as everyday conversations and require careful preparation and execution.

The importance of crucial conversations in Agile development

In Agile development, crucial conversations are critical for ensuring that the team is aligned in terms of goals, priorities, and expectations. These conversations can help to identify and address issues early on, prevent misunderstandings, and improve team dynamics. By having open and honest communication, the team can make better decisions and deliver high-quality products that meet the user's needs.

Techniques for holding crucial conversations

There are several key techniques for holding crucial conversations effectively. First, it's essential to create a safe environment where everyone feels comfortable sharing their thoughts and opinions. This can involve setting ground rules, acknowledging each other's perspectives, and avoiding blame and judgment.

Active listening is another critical technique for holding crucial conversations. This involves listening to understand, not just responding. It's essential to ask clarifying questions, summarize what you've heard, and validate the other person's emotions.

Finally, making your point of view clear is critical in crucial conversations. It's important to express your thoughts and feelings in a way that is respectful and non-confrontational. This can involve using "I" statements instead of "you" statements and avoiding absolutes.

Steps for preparing for a crucial conversation

Effective preparation is key to holding a successful crucial conversation. Before the conversation, it's essential to understand your own emotions and goals, as well as the other party's perspectives and interests. This can involve identifying your triggers, reflecting on your assumptions, and considering the other person's motivations and concerns.

Examples of crucial conversations in Agile development

Crucial conversations can arise in many different contexts in Agile development. For example, discussing product priorities, addressing team dynamics, and providing feedback on performance can all be crucial conversations. It's essential to handle these conversations with care and attention, using the techniques and steps we've discussed.

In conclusion, crucial conversations are an essential part of Agile development. By understanding what constitutes a crucial conversation, the importance of these discussions, and the techniques and steps for holding them effectively, you can improve communication and collaboration within your team, leading to better product outcomes.

Concrete examples of ways to work with stakeholders

Here are some examples of ways to work with stakeholders:

- **User interviews and surveys**: Conducting user interviews and surveys is a valuable way to gather feedback directly from stakeholders. For example, a product manager working on a mobile banking app might organize user interviews to understand user preferences for the app's interface, features, and overall user experience. The feedback gathered from stakeholders can then be used to inform decision-making and prioritize future development efforts.

- **Collaborative workshops**: Organizing collaborative workshops brings together stakeholders from various departments to collectively brainstorm and generate ideas. For instance, a product manager facilitating a workshop for a new e-commerce platform might invite stakeholders from marketing, sales, design, and development to collaborate on defining the platform's key features, target audience, and business goals. The workshop can foster cross-functional collaboration and alignment between stakeholders.

- **Usability testing sessions**: Conducting usability testing sessions involves inviting stakeholders to interact with a working prototype or an early version of the product to gather real-time feedback. For example, a user experience designer might organize a usability testing session for a web application and observe how stakeholders navigate through the interface, complete tasks, and provide feedback on areas of improvement. Usability testing provides valuable insights into the user experience and helps identify potential usability issues.

- **Sprint reviews**: Sprint reviews provide an opportunity to showcase the progress of the product to stakeholders and gather their feedback. During a sprint review, the development team presents the completed work from the iteration to stakeholders, demonstrating the new features and functionality. Stakeholders can provide feedback, ask questions, and suggest changes based on their observations. This feedback informs future iterations and helps align the product with stakeholder expectations.

- **Stakeholder feedback sessions**: Setting up dedicated feedback sessions with stakeholders allows for open and constructive discussions about the product. These sessions can be in the form of regular meetings or workshops where stakeholders have the opportunity to share their thoughts, concerns, and suggestions. For instance, a product owner might organize a quarterly stakeholder feedback session to discuss the product roadmap, gather input on new feature requests, and address any emerging issues.

- **Collaborative product management tools**: Utilizing collaborative product management tools can enhance communication and engagement among stakeholders. These tools provide a centralized platform where stakeholders can access product updates, track progress, provide feedback, and collaborate on tasks. For example, using a product management tool such as Jira or Trello allows stakeholders to stay informed about the product's status, contribute to discussions, and monitor the progress of user stories.

These examples illustrate practical ways to work with stakeholders, involving them in the development process, gathering feedback, and fostering collaboration. By actively engaging stakeholders throughout the project, teams can build stronger relationships, align expectations, and deliver products that truly meet stakeholder needs.

There is a common saying in the field of product management and software development: "There is no such thing as best practices, only best practices in context." This statement emphasizes the idea that what works well in one situation may not necessarily be effective in another. It recognizes that the best approach or practice depends on the unique context and circumstances of a product or organization.

Here are a few key points to consider when it comes to best practices in context:

- **Context matters**: Every product or organization operates within a specific context that includes factors such as industry, company culture, team dynamics, product goals, and constraints. What may be considered a best practice in one context may not be suitable or applicable in another. It is important to consider the unique aspects of your product or organization and adapt practices accordingly.

- **Tailoring to fit**: Rather than blindly adopting best practices, it is crucial to tailor them to suit your specific needs. This involves understanding the principles behind the practice and adapting them to align with your context. This way, you can leverage the value of best practices while ensuring they are suitable for your unique situation.

- **Continuous learning and improvement**: Instead of relying solely on predefined best practices, it is important to foster a culture of continuous learning and improvement. Encourage experimentation, embrace feedback, and be open to adjusting practices based on the outcomes. This iterative approach allows for adaptation and optimization over time.

- **Experimentation and adaptation**: Recognize that what works today may not work tomorrow. Embrace a mindset of experimentation and be willing to adapt practices as needed. This requires being flexible and responsive to changing circumstances, emerging technologies, and evolving customer needs.

- **Collaboration and shared learning**: Engage in knowledge-sharing and collaboration within your organization and industry. Learn from others' experiences, participate in communities of practice, attend conferences, and keep up with industry trends. By sharing insights and learning from others, you can gain valuable perspectives and identify practices that may be relevant to your context.

Remember, while best practices can offer guidance and insights, they should not be seen as rigid rules to follow blindly. Adaptability, critical thinking, and a focus on continuous improvement are key to finding and applying the most effective practices in your specific context.

Best practices for working with stakeholders

Here are some best practices for working with stakeholders:

- **Establishing clear communication channels**: Set up effective communication channels to ensure smooth and timely information flow between the development team and stakeholders. This can include regular meetings, email updates, product management tools, or collaboration platforms. Clear and transparent communication helps keep stakeholders informed and engaged throughout the project.

- **Defining roles and responsibilities**: Clearly define the roles and responsibilities of stakeholders of the product. This helps set expectations and ensures that stakeholders understand their involvement and contributions. Assign specific roles, such as product owner, user representative, or sponsor, to stakeholders based on their expertise and interests.

- **Involving stakeholders early and continuously**: Involve stakeholders from the early stages of the project and maintain their engagement throughout the development process. Seek their input during the requirements gathering, user story creation, and design phases. Regularly solicit feedback and involve stakeholders in decision-making to ensure their needs and perspectives are considered.

- **Fostering collaboration and empathy**: Encourage collaboration and empathy among stakeholders and the development team. Create a safe and inclusive environment where stakeholders feel comfortable expressing their opinions, concerns, and ideas. Foster a culture of mutual respect and understanding to facilitate productive discussions and effective collaboration.

- **Prioritizing and managing expectations**: Prioritize stakeholders' needs and align the product goals with their expectations. Conduct regular prioritization exercises to ensure that the most valuable features and requirements are addressed first. Manage expectations by providing realistic timelines and clearly communicating any constraints or limitations.

- **Providing regular updates and progress reports**: Keep stakeholders informed about the product's progress through regular updates and progress reports. This helps maintain transparency and ensures that stakeholders are aware of the product's status, milestones, and any changes in direction. Use visual aids, such as dashboards or visualizations, to present information clearly and concisely.

- **Embracing feedback and iterating**: Embrace stakeholder feedback as an opportunity for improvement. Actively listen to their suggestions, concerns, and criticisms, and take the appropriate actions to address them. Use feedback to drive iterative development and continuous improvement, ensuring that the product evolves based on stakeholder needs and market demands.

- **Building strong relationships**: Cultivate strong relationships with stakeholders by demonstrating trust, respect, and transparency. Foster open lines of communication, actively seek their involvement, and show appreciation for their contributions. Strong relationships contribute to smoother collaboration, increased stakeholder engagement, and a more successful outcome.

- **Managing conflict constructively**: Conflict may arise between stakeholders with differing perspectives or priorities. Address conflicts constructively by facilitating open discussions, seeking common ground, and finding win-win solutions. Act as a mediator or facilitator to help stakeholders resolve conflicts and maintain a positive working relationship.

- **Evaluating and adjusting**: Continuously evaluate the effectiveness of stakeholder engagement strategies and adjust your approach as needed. Regularly seek feedback from stakeholders about their experience and make improvements based on their input. Adapt your communication and collaboration methods to better meet the needs and preferences of stakeholders.

By following these best practices, product managers and development teams can effectively collaborate with stakeholders, foster meaningful relationships, and ensure successful product outcomes that meet stakeholders' expectations.

Summary

In this chapter, we delved into working with stakeholders, including identifying and categorizing stakeholders, managing stakeholder expectations, and keeping them engaged throughout product development. Next, we explored collaboration techniques such as active listening, empathy, and effective communication, while the next section covered conflict resolution and the importance of crucial conversations. Then, we discussed negotiation techniques, including understanding the other party's perspective and interests and finding a mutually beneficial solution.

Communicating user stories effectively to different teams is critical for the success of an Agile development product. By understanding the roles and responsibilities of different stakeholders, creating a shared understanding of user stories, breaking down complex user stories, collaborating effectively, and tailoring communication to different team members, we can ensure that everyone is on the same page and working toward a common goal.

In further chapters, such as those on communication, conflict resolution, and stakeholder engagement, these skills and tools will be essential for success. Effective communication requires emotional intelligence and empathy, while conflict resolution requires self-regulation and social skills. Equally, stakeholder engagement requires not only effective communication but also the ability to understand and manage the emotions and expectations of stakeholders.

Overall, the lessons in this chapter on emotional intelligence lay the foundation for success in Agile development products and beyond. In the next chapter, we will dive deeper into the process of user story refinement and explore how continuous improvement can help teams refine their work and stay on track. We will also discuss the benefits of continuous improvement and how it can help teams to achieve their goals.

Questions

1. What are some common challenges that product managers and product owners face when working with stakeholders?

2. What are some techniques for identifying stakeholders and their needs?

3. How can you effectively communicate with stakeholders?

4. What are some strategies for managing stakeholder expectations?

5. How can you handle conflicts with stakeholders effectively?

6. How can you keep stakeholders engaged throughout the project?

Answers

1. Some common challenges that product managers and product owners face when working with stakeholders include conflicting priorities, limited resources, stakeholder resistance to change, and difficulty in aligning stakeholder expectations with product goals.

2. Techniques for identifying stakeholders and their needs include conducting stakeholder interviews, creating stakeholder personas, using surveys and feedback forms, and analyzing user data. It's important to involve stakeholders early on in the project to ensure that their needs are understood and addressed.

3. To effectively communicate with stakeholders, it's important to understand their communication styles and preferences and tailor your communication accordingly. It's also important to provide regular updates, be transparent about product progress and challenges, and actively listen to stakeholder feedback. Using clear and concise language and visual aids can also help to effectively communicate complex information.

4. Strategies for managing stakeholder expectations include setting clear product goals and timelines, involving stakeholders in the product planning process, prioritizing stakeholder needs, and providing regular updates on product progress. It's important to be transparent about any changes or challenges that may arise during the product and work collaboratively with stakeholders to find solutions.

5. Handling conflicts with stakeholders effectively involves identifying the root cause of the conflict, actively listening to stakeholder concerns, and finding a mutually beneficial solution. It's important to remain calm and professional and to use active listening and effective communication techniques to understand and address stakeholder concerns. Seeking mediation or involving a neutral third party may also be necessary in some cases.

6. To keep stakeholders engaged throughout the project, it's important to involve them in the product planning process, provide regular updates on product progress, and actively seek their feedback and input. Offering opportunities for stakeholder engagement, such as user testing or focus groups, can also help to keep stakeholders invested in the product.

User Story Refinement and Continuous Improvement

In this chapter, we will dive into the process of refining user stories and continuously improving the product. Refinement is a critical step in Agile development that involves revisiting and updating existing user stories to ensure they meet the needs of the customer and the team. Continuous improvement is also vital as it ensures the product is always growing and evolving to meet the changing needs of the user.

Understanding the importance of user story refinement and continuous improvement is crucial in Agile development. By refining user stories, the development team can ensure that the stories are well defined, actionable, and aligned with the needs of the users. Continuous improvement, on the other hand, allows the team to enhance the product over time by incorporating feedback and making iterative refinements. In this chapter, we will explore the process of refining user stories and continuously improving the product. We will discuss the various techniques and tools that can be used to refine user stories, such as story mapping, backlog grooming, and collaborative discussions with stakeholders. Additionally, we will delve into the concept of continuous improvement and how it can be integrated into the Agile development process.

Throughout the chapter, we will address the challenges commonly encountered in user story refinement and continuous improvement, and provide best practices to overcome them. By the end of this chapter, you will have a solid understanding of the importance of user story refinement and continuous improvement, and you will be equipped with practical knowledge and strategies to effectively refine user stories and drive continuous improvement in your Agile products.

In this chapter, we're going to cover the following main topics:

- The importance of user story refinement and continuous improvement in Agile development
- The process of refining user stories
- Techniques and tools for refining user stories

- The importance of continuous improvement

- Challenges and best practices associated with user story refinement and continuous improvement

The importance of user story refinement and continuous improvement in Agile development

User story refinement and continuous improvement are essential components of Agile development. They ensure that the product remains aligned with the customer's needs and expectations while adapting to changing circumstances. By continuously refining user stories and improving the product, the team can deliver high-quality software that provides value to the end users.

In Agile development, requirements are never set in stone. Instead, they evolve as the team gains a better understanding of the user's needs and the market landscape. User story refinement allows the team to update and adjust user stories based on feedback from stakeholders, customer input, and the team's own experience. This iterative process ensures that the product backlog is always up to date and accurately reflects the priorities and requirements of the product.

Continuous improvement, on the other hand, focuses on enhancing the overall quality of the product by regularly evaluating its performance and making necessary adjustments. This includes analyzing user feedback, identifying areas for improvement, and implementing changes to the product in a timely manner.

User story refinement, also known as **backlog refinement**, is the process of reviewing, updating, and improving user stories to ensure they are clear, concise, and testable. It is essential for maintaining an up-to-date and prioritized product backlog that aligns with the product's goals, customer needs, and business objectives. The refinement process typically involves the following:

- Reviewing and prioritizing the product backlog for consistency and relevance

- Gathering feedback from customers, stakeholders, and team members

- Revising and improving user stories based on feedback and product requirements

- Estimating the effort required to complete each user story

- Collaborating with the team to foster a shared understanding of user stories and product goals

Following this comprehensive alignment on user stories and product objectives, our next focus will be on the concept and importance of continuous improvement. This approach is key to ensuring our team's processes and outputs constantly evolve, grow, and adapt to the shifting demands of our product and industry.

Understanding continuous improvement

Continuous improvement is the ongoing process of optimizing team performance, processes, and product quality by reflecting on past experiences, learning from them, and implementing changes. Key aspects of continuous improvement include the following:

- Conducting regular retrospectives to identify areas for improvement

- Experimenting with new techniques, tools, and processes

- Tracking and analyzing performance metrics

- Fostering a culture of ongoing learning and growth within the team

The impact of user story refinement and continuous improvement on Agile development

User story refinement and continuous improvement have a profound impact on the Agile development process, providing several benefits:

- **Improved prioritization**: Refined user stories enable teams to prioritize their work more effectively, focusing on high-value features that deliver the most significant impact to customers

- **Enhanced clarity and understanding**: Clear, concise, and testable user stories help teams better understand the product requirements, reducing the risk of miscommunication and costly rework

- **Streamlined development process**: Regular refinement and continuous improvement lead to more efficient development processes, helping teams deliver high-quality products faster and more reliably

- **Higher customer satisfaction**: By continuously updating the product backlog and improving processes, Agile teams can better meet customer needs and expectations, resulting in higher customer satisfaction

- **Greater adaptability**: Continuous improvement allows teams to be more responsive to changes in customer needs, market conditions, or product requirements, ensuring the product remains relevant and competitive

Emphasizing the importance of user story refinement and continuous improvement

To truly benefit from user story refinement and continuous improvement, Agile teams must do the following:

- Actively solicit customer feedback on their experience with user stories

- Allocate dedicated time for refinement and improvement activities

- Encourage open communication, collaboration, and active participation from all team members

- Emphasize the value of learning from past experiences and embracing change

- Utilize a variety of techniques, tools, and practices to support the refinement and improvement processes

User story refinement and continuous improvement are indispensable practices in Agile development, driving product success and team performance. By understanding their importance and incorporating these practices into their development process, Agile teams can deliver high-quality products that meet or exceed customer needs and expectations. Emphasizing the significance of refinement and continuous improvement will ultimately lead to a more streamlined, efficient, and adaptive Agile development process.

The process of refining user stories

Refining user stories is an ongoing activity throughout the Agile development process. It typically involves the following steps:

1. **Reviewing existing user stories**: The team examines the current user stories in the product backlog to ensure they are clear, concise, and meet the **INVEST** criteria (**Independent**, **Negotiable**, **Valuable**, **Estimable**, **Small**, and **Testable**).

2. **Identifying gaps and inconsistencies**: The team looks for any missing information, discrepancies, or ambiguities in the user stories that might hinder the development process.

3. **Prioritizing user stories**: The team evaluates the importance of each user story based on factors such as business value, risk, and dependencies. This helps to determine the order in which user stories should be addressed during development.

4. **Updating user stories**: The team updates and refines user stories based on the feedback received from stakeholders and customers, as well as their own insights.

5. **Estimating effort**: The team collaborates to estimate the effort required to complete each refined user story. This allows better planning and resource allocation.

User story refinement is an essential practice in Agile development that ensures the product backlog stays relevant, clear, and prioritized. This section will discuss the process of refining user stories, the steps involved, and the benefits of engaging in regular refinement sessions. By the end of this section, you will have a thorough understanding of the process of refining user stories and how it contributes to a successful Agile product.

Overview of user story refinement

User story refinement, also known as **backlog refinement**, is the process of reviewing, updating, and improving user stories to ensure they are clear, concise, and testable. The primary objectives of user story refinement are as follows:

- Maintain an up-to-date and prioritized product backlog
- Ensure user stories are well defined, easy to understand, and ready for development
- Foster communication and collaboration within the team, promoting shared understanding and ownership of the product

Steps in the user story refinement process

Refining user stories is an ongoing process that should be conducted throughout the project. The process typically involves the following steps:

1. Review the product backlog.
2. Gather feedback.
3. Refine user stories.
4. Estimate effort.
5. Collaborate with the team.

Review the product backlog

Regularly review and update the product backlog to ensure that it aligns with the product's goals and priorities. Remove or deprioritize user stories that are no longer relevant and add new user stories as needed.

Gather feedback

Seek input from customers, stakeholders, and team members to better understand their needs and expectations. This feedback can help identify gaps, inconsistencies, or potential improvements in the user stories.

Refine user stories

Revise and improve user stories based on the feedback received, ensuring that they are clear, concise, and testable. Break down large or complex user stories into smaller, more manageable tasks, and ensure that each user story aligns with the INVEST criteria.

Estimate effort

Assign relative effort levels to each user story, helping the team to prioritize their work and plan future iterations. Use techniques such as planning poker or T-shirt sizing to facilitate estimation and foster team collaboration.

Collaborate with the team

Engage in discussions with the team to clarify any doubts and foster a shared understanding of the user stories. Encourage open communication and active participation from all team members during the refinement process.

Best practices for user story refinement

To maximize the benefits of user story refinement, consider the following best practices:

- Allocate dedicated time for refinement sessions, ideally between 5% and 10% of the team's capacity
- Schedule refinement sessions regularly, such as once a week or once every two weeks, depending on the product's needs and team preferences
- Encourage open communication, collaboration, and active participation from all team members
- Utilize a variety of techniques and tools to support the refinement process, such as story mapping, planning poker, or the **Definition of Ready (DoR)** criteria

Techniques and tools for refining user stories

There are several techniques and tools available to help teams refine user stories effectively. Some of these are as follows:

- **User story mapping**: This technique helps the team visualize the user's journey through the product and identify any gaps or inconsistencies in the user stories
- **Story splitting**: This involves breaking down large user stories into small, more manageable pieces that can be developed and delivered more quickly
- **Planning Poker**: This is a consensus-based estimation technique that helps the team estimate the effort required to complete each user story
- **Online collaboration tools**: Tools such as Trello, Jira, and Asana can be used to manage, prioritize, and refine user stories efficiently

Refining user stories is an essential part of Agile development that ensures the product backlog remains relevant, clear, and prioritized. Several techniques and tools can facilitate this process, helping teams to create well-defined, easy-to-understand, and ready-for-development user stories. This section will explore various techniques and tools used for refining user stories, providing practical examples and guidance on how to incorporate them into your Agile products.

Story mapping

Story mapping is a visual representation of the user journey through the product, helping teams identify gaps, prioritize user stories, and get a holistic view of the product backlog. To create a story map, follow these steps:

1. Identify the main user activities or goals.

2. Break down each activity into smaller tasks or user stories.

3. Arrange the user stories in a top-down and left-to-right hierarchy based on their priority and sequence.

4. Use the story map to discuss, prioritize, and refine user stories during refinement sessions.

Definition of Ready (DoR)

The DoR is a set of criteria that a user story must meet before it can be considered ready for development. Establishing a DoR ensures that user stories are clear, concise, and testable, minimizing the risk of miscommunication or rework. A DoR might include the following criteria:

-   User story aligns with the INVEST criteria

-   Acceptance criteria are clearly defined

-   Dependencies are identified and resolved

-   The user story is estimated and prioritized

Planning poker

Planning poker is a consensus-based estimation technique that helps teams assign relative effort levels to user stories. A planning poker session looks as follows:

1. Each team member receives a set of cards with numbers representing the Fibonacci sequence (e.g., 1, 2, 3, 5, 8, 13).

2. The product owner or Scrum Master presents a user story and its acceptance criteria.

3. Each team member privately selects a card representing their estimate of the effort required to complete the user story.

4. All team members reveal their cards simultaneously.

5. The team discusses the estimates, focusing on any significant discrepancies, and repeats the process until a consensus is reached.

User story splitting

User story splitting involves breaking down large or complex user stories into smaller, more manageable tasks. This technique helps teams create user stories that are easier to understand, estimate, and develop. Some common methods for splitting user stories are as follows:

- **Workflow steps**: Break down the user story based on the sequence of tasks or steps the user must complete

- **Business rules**: Split the user story into separate stories for each business rule or condition

- **Data variations**: Divide the user story into smaller stories based on different data inputs or outputs

- **Operations**: Split the user story into smaller stories based on the operations or actions the user performs (e.g., create, read, update, delete)

Collaboration tools and visual management

Using collaboration tools and visual management techniques can help teams efficiently refine user stories and maintain an up-to-date product backlog. Some popular tools and techniques are as follows:

- **Digital tools**: Use digital tools such as Trello, Jira, or Asana to manage and refine user stories, estimate effort, and track progress

- **Physical boards**: Create a physical board with sticky notes or index cards to represent user stories, allowing the team to visualize and interact with the product backlog during refinement sessions

- **Information radiators**: Display key information related to the product backlog and refinement process, such as story maps, DoR criteria, or estimation guidelines, in a visible location for easy reference

Employing various techniques and tools for refining user stories can significantly improve the clarity, consistency, and prioritization of the product backlog, ultimately leading to more successful Agile products.

The importance of continuous improvement

Continuous improvement is vital in Agile development to ensure the product's ongoing success. It involves the following:

- Regularly reviewing and analyzing user feedback and product performance metrics
- Identifying areas for improvement and implementing changes to the product
- Encouraging a culture of learning, experimentation, and innovation within the team

Continuous improvement is a critical aspect of Agile development that focuses on the ongoing optimization of team performance, processes, and product quality. This section will discuss the importance of continuous improvement, its benefits, and how it contributes to the success of Agile products. By the end of this section, you will have a deep understanding of the significance of continuous improvement and its role in Agile development.

Understanding continuous improvement

Continuous improvement is the ongoing process of identifying areas for improvement by learning from past experiences and implementations. Key aspects of continuous improvement include the following:

- Reflecting on past experiences and lessons learned
- Experimenting with new techniques, tools, and processes
- Tracking and analyzing performance metrics
- Fostering a culture of ongoing learning and growth within the team

Benefits of continuous improvement

Embracing continuous improvement in Agile development provides several benefits:

- **Enhanced efficiency and effectiveness**: Continuous improvement helps identify and eliminate bottlenecks, redundancies, and waste in the development process, leading to more efficient and effective workflows
- **Improved product quality**: By regularly reviewing and optimizing processes and practices, teams can deliver higher-quality products that better meet customer needs and expectations
- **Increased adaptability**: Continuous improvement enables teams to be more responsive to changes in customer needs, market conditions, or product requirements, ensuring the product remains relevant and competitive
- **Stronger team collaboration and communication**: Fostering a culture of continuous improvement encourages open communication, collaboration, and shared ownership of the product and processes, leading to a more cohesive and high-performing team

- **Higher customer satisfaction**: Regularly reviewing and improving processes based on customer feedback and needs helps ensure that the product stays aligned with customer expectations, resulting in increased satisfaction and loyalty

Continuous improvement in Agile development

In Agile development, continuous improvement is typically facilitated through practices such as the following:

- Regular retrospectives: Conduct retrospectives at the end of each iteration to reflect on the team's performance, identify areas for improvement, and agree on action items to address in the next iteration

- Experimentation: Encourage the team to experiment with new techniques, tools, and processes, and evaluate their effectiveness based on metrics and feedback

- Metrics and feedback: Collect and analyze performance metrics, customer feedback, and stakeholder input to identify areas for improvement and track the impact of changes

- Continuous learning: Foster a culture of ongoing learning and growth by providing opportunities for team members to acquire new skills, attend workshops, and share knowledge with one another

Best practices for continuous improvement

To maximize the benefits of continuous improvement, consider the following best practices:

- Encourage open communication, collaboration, and active participation from all team members

- Set realistic, measurable goals for improvement efforts to track progress and demonstrate results

- Prioritize improvement initiatives based on their potential impact on team performance, product quality, and customer satisfaction

- Regularly review and update improvement plans to ensure they remain relevant and aligned with the team's goals and objectives

- Celebrate successes and learn from failures, fostering a culture of continuous learning and growth

The importance of continuous improvement in Agile development cannot be overstated. By embracing continuous improvement, Agile teams can optimize their processes, enhance product quality, and adapt to changing needs, leading to more successful products and satisfied customers. By understanding the significance of continuous improvement and incorporating best practices into their development process, Agile teams can foster a culture of ongoing learning, growth, and excellence.

Challenges and best practices associated with user story refinement and continuous improvement

Some challenges in user story refinement and continuous improvement are as follows:

- **Resistance to change**: Team members may be hesitant to revise user stories or make changes to the product

- **Inadequate communication**: Poor communication among team members can lead to misunderstandings and conflicts during the refinement process

To overcome these challenges, consider the following best practices:

- Foster a culture of openness and collaboration within the team

- Encourage regular communication and feedback from stakeholders and customers

- Allocate sufficient time for user story refinement and continuous improvement

User story refinement and continuous improvement are essential aspects of Agile development that contribute to product success. However, teams may face challenges in implementing these practices effectively. This section will discuss the common challenges associated with user story refinement and continuous improvement and provide best practices to address these challenges. By the end of this section, you will be equipped with practical solutions to overcome obstacles and enhance your Agile development process.

Challenges in user story refinement

- Ambiguity and lack of clarity: User stories that are vague, incomplete, or poorly defined can lead to miscommunication, rework, and delays in the development process

- Inconsistent prioritization: Conflicting priorities within the team or organization can make it difficult to prioritize user stories effectively, resulting in inefficient allocation of resources and potential delays

- Overly large or complex user stories: Large or complex user stories can be challenging to understand, estimate, and develop, leading to delays and increased risk of errors

- Insufficient team involvement: Limited participation from team members in the refinement process can result in a lack of shared understanding and ownership of the user stories

Best practices for user story refinement

- Establish clear guidelines and criteria: Define and communicate guidelines and criteria for creating and refining user stories, such as the INVEST criteria and the DoR

- Foster open communication and collaboration: Encourage active participation from all team members during refinement sessions, promoting shared understanding and ownership of the user stories

- Break down large or complex user stories: Use techniques such as user story splitting to break down large or complex user stories into smaller, more manageable tasks

- Regularly review and update the product backlog: Schedule regular refinement sessions to review and update the product backlog, ensuring it remains aligned with the product's goals and priorities

Challenges in continuous improvement

- Resistance to change: Team members may resist adopting new practices, tools, or processes, making it difficult to implement continuous improvement initiatives

- Lack of clear goals and metrics: Without clear goals and measurable metrics, it can be challenging to track the progress and impact of continuous improvement efforts

- Insufficient time and resources: Teams may struggle to allocate sufficient time and resources to continuous improvement activities, resulting in a lack of focus on improvement initiatives

- Inadequate feedback loops: Ineffective feedback mechanisms can hinder the team's ability to identify areas for improvement and evaluate the impact of changes

- Changing priorities or even external conditions

Best practices for continuous improvement

- Foster a culture of learning and growth: Encourage a growth mindset within the team, promoting open communication, collaboration, and continuous learning

- Set clear goals and measurable metrics: Define realistic, measurable goals for improvement efforts and track progress using relevant metrics

- Allocate dedicated time for continuous improvement: Schedule regular retrospectives and allocate dedicated time for improvement activities to ensure they remain a priority

- Establish effective feedback loops: Collect and analyze feedback from team members, customers, and stakeholders to identify areas for improvement and evaluate the impact of changes

By adopting these best practices, teams can create a more effective and collaborative environment, fostering a culture of continuous improvement and excellence.

User story refinement example

Imagine a team is working on a product to create an online shopping website. One of the initial user stories created is as follows:

"As a customer, I want to search for products so that I can find what I need quickly."

During the refinement process, the team collaborates to break down and improve the user story based on their understanding of the product requirements and customer feedback:

"As a customer, I want to search for products by entering keywords, choosing categories, and applying filters, so that I can find the exact product I'm looking for easily."

This refined user story is now more specific, detailed, and testable, providing the development team with a clearer understanding of the expected functionality.

Continuous improvement example

Suppose the team has completed a few iterations of the online shopping website product and conducted retrospectives after each iteration. They identified that the time taken to review and merge code changes has been consistently increasing, leading to delays in the development process.

To address this issue, the team decides to experiment with new approaches for code review and integration. They implement a new code review process that involves peer reviews and automated checks using a static code analysis tool. In addition, they introduce **Continuous Integration** (**CI**) practices to build and test the code automatically after every commit.

After implementing these changes, the team monitors their performance metrics and observes a significant reduction in the time taken for code reviews and merging. This continuous improvement effort not only optimizes the development process but also enhances the overall quality and stability of the product.

Summary

In this chapter, we covered the importance of user story refinement and continuous improvement in Agile development, emphasizing their vital role in delivering high-quality products that meet customer needs. We explored the processes, techniques, and tools for refining user stories, as well as the benefits and challenges associated with continuous improvement. The chapter also provided best practices to address these challenges and improve the Agile development process.

The key lessons covered include the following:

- The significance of user story refinement and continuous improvement in Agile development
- The process of refining user stories and various techniques and tools that can aid in this process

- The importance of continuous improvement in enhancing efficiency, product quality, and team collaboration

- Challenges and best practices associated with user story refinement and continuous improvement

Mastering these skills will enable readers to create well-defined, easy-to-understand user stories, optimize their Agile development process, and ultimately deliver better products to their customers.

In the next chapter, we will delve into user stories in practice. This is the next natural step from user story refinement and continuous improvement, as user stories in practice will further illuminate the application of the concepts covered in this chapter.

Questions

1. What is the importance of user story refinement in Agile development?

2. What are some common techniques for refining user stories?

3. What are the benefits of continuous improvement in Agile development?

4. What are some challenges associated with user story refinement and continuous improvement?

5. How can teams address the challenges in user story refinement and continuous improvement?

6. What is the role of retrospectives in continuous improvement?

Answers

1. User story refinement is important in Agile development because it ensures that the product backlog remains relevant, clear, and prioritized. It helps teams create well-defined, easy-to-understand, and ready-for-development user stories, minimizing the risk of miscommunication, rework, and delays in the development process.

2. Some common techniques for refining user stories include story mapping, using a **Definition of Ready (DoR)**, planning poker for effort estimation, and user story splitting based on workflow steps, business rules, data variations, or operations.

3. Continuous improvement offers several benefits in Agile development, such as enhanced efficiency and effectiveness, improved product quality, increased adaptability to changing needs, stronger team collaboration and communication, and higher customer satisfaction.

4. Some challenges associated with user story refinement include ambiguity and lack of clarity in user stories, inconsistent prioritization, overly large or complex user stories, and insufficient team involvement. Challenges associated with continuous improvement include resistance to change, lack of clear goals and metrics, insufficient time and resources, and inadequate feedback loops.

5.   To address the challenges in user story refinement, teams can establish clear guidelines and criteria, foster open communication and collaboration, break down large or complex user stories, and regularly review and update the product backlog. To address challenges in continuous improvement, teams can foster a culture of learning and growth, set clear goals and measurable metrics, allocate dedicated time for continuous improvement, and establish effective feedback loops.

6.   Retrospectives play a crucial role in continuous improvement, as they provide an opportunity for teams to reflect on their performance, identify areas for improvement, and agree on action items to address in the next iteration. Regular retrospectives help teams learn from past experiences and make data-driven decisions to optimize their processes and practices.

7

User Stories in Practice

Welcome to this chapter on *user stories in practice!* User stories are valuable tools for capturing requirements, communicating with stakeholders, and guiding the development process. By understanding how to effectively create, refine, and use user stories, you will be able to enhance your product development workflow and deliver successful outcomes.

In this chapter, we will explore case studies for the following main topics:

- Case study – creating effective user stories for a task management application
- Case study – user story mapping for a social media platform
- Case study – building a task management app
- Case study – collaborative refinement and iterative development
- Case study – validating user stories
- Case study – iterative release and continuous improvement
- Case study – estimating user stories for an e-commerce platform
- Case study – splitting and refining user stories for a task management application
- Case study – defining acceptance criteria and the definition of done for an e-commerce website

By the end of this chapter, you will have gained practical knowledge and skills in creating effective user stories, refining them through continuous improvement, and making informed decisions through estimation and prioritization. You will be equipped with the tools and techniques to collaborate effectively with your team, engage stakeholders, and drive successful agile development products. So, let's dive in and uncover the power of user stories in practice!

Case study – creating effective user stories for a task management application

In this case study, we will explore the process of creating effective user stories for a task management application called **TaskMaster**. The goal of TaskMaster is to provide users with a seamless and intuitive platform for managing their tasks, deadlines, and priorities. We will follow the journey of a product team as they work on defining and refining user stories to ensure the development of a successful and user-centric application:

1. Understanding user needs
2. Defining epics and themes
3. Creating user stories
4. Prioritizing and refining user stories

Understanding user needs

The product team conducts user research and interviews to gain insights into the target users' needs and pain points. They identify key personas, such as busy professionals and students, who will benefit from an efficient task management tool. By empathizing with the users, the team gains a deeper understanding of their motivations and expectations.

Identifying key personas

When writing user stories, it's essential to identify key personas that represent the target users of the product. For example, if you're developing a task management tool, you might identify personas such as busy professionals and students. By understanding the characteristics, needs, and goals of these personas, the development team can align their efforts with the users' requirements and expectations.

Empathizing with users

Empathy plays a crucial role in Agile product development. By putting themselves in the users' shoes, the team gains a deeper understanding of their motivations, pain points, and desired outcomes. This understanding helps shape the features and functionality of the product to address the specific needs of the target users. Through techniques such as user research, interviews, and usability testing, the team can gather valuable insights and feedback to inform the development process.

During the empathizing phase, the team may conduct interviews or surveys to gather qualitative and quantitative data about the users' preferences, habits, and pain points. This information serves as a foundation for creating user stories and shaping the product vision.

The process of identifying key personas and empathizing with users is an iterative one. The team continuously gathers feedback and validates its assumptions through user testing and feedback sessions. This iterative approach allows for the refinement and evolution of the user story as the team learns more about the users and their needs.

By incorporating the perspectives and insights gained from identifying key personas and empathizing with users, the user story becomes a powerful tool for aligning the development team's efforts with the users' expectations. It ensures that the product is designed and developed with the user in mind, resulting in a more user-centric and successful product.

Identifying user needs

To effectively identify user needs, the development team can employ various research techniques and tools. This may include conducting user interviews, surveys, usability testing, and analyzing user behavior data. The goal is to gather insights into user preferences, pain points, and desired outcomes:

- **User interviews**: One-on-one interviews with potential users can provide valuable qualitative data. Through open-ended questions and active listening, the team can uncover users' motivations, challenges, and expectations. These insights help in creating user stories that address their specific needs.

- **Surveys**: Surveys enable gathering quantitative data from a larger user base. By asking targeted questions, the team can gather insights into user preferences, usage patterns, and satisfaction levels. Surveys can be conducted online or in person, depending on the target audience.

- **Usability testing**: Usability testing involves observing users as they interact with a prototype or the existing product. This hands-on approach helps the team understand how users navigate the interface, identify pain points, and uncover areas for improvement. Usability testing can be conducted in a controlled lab setting or remotely.

- **Analyzing user behavior data**: By analyzing user behavior data, such as website analytics or product usage metrics, the team can gain insights into how users engage with the product. This data can reveal patterns, identify popular features, and highlight areas of improvement.

Throughout the process, it's crucial to maintain a user-centric mindset and actively involve users in the research and feedback process. By understanding their needs, the team can create user stories that accurately reflect their goals and expectations.

The insights gathered from these research activities form the foundation for identifying user needs and shaping user stories. It's important to regularly revisit and update these user needs as the product progresses, ensuring that the product remains aligned with the evolving requirements of the users.

By employing these research techniques and actively involving users, the development team can gain a deep understanding of their needs and create effective user stories that address those needs. This user-centered approach leads to the development of a product that truly resonates with its intended users and meets their expectations.

Defining epics and themes

Based on the user research, the product team identifies high-level epics and themes that represent the major functionalities and features of the TaskMaster application. These epics, such as task creation, task organization, and deadline tracking, serve as a starting point for creating user stories.

Creating user stories

The team collaborates to create user stories using the popular `"As a user, I want, so that"` format. They ensure that each user story is concise, specific, and focused on delivering value to the user. For example, a user story could be `"As a busy professional, I want to set priority levels for tasks, so that I can efficiently manage my workload."`.

Case study – user story mapping for a social media platform

In this case study, we will explore the process of using user story mapping to design and develop a social media platform called **Connectify**. The goal of Connectify is to provide users with a seamless and engaging platform for connecting with friends, sharing content, and discovering new interests. We will follow the journey of a product team as they utilize user story mapping to plan and prioritize the development of Connectify.

Defining the product vision

The product team conducts market research and identifies the need for a user-friendly and feature-rich social media platform. They envision Connectify as a platform that fosters meaningful connections, encourages content creation, and promotes user engagement.

Gathering user insights

The team conducts user interviews, surveys, and usability tests to gain deep insights into the target audience's needs, preferences, and pain points. They identify key user personas and user types, such as young professionals and hobbyists, to represent the diverse user base of Connectify.

Creating the user story map

The product team collaborates to create a user story map, a visual representation of user stories arranged in a logical flow. They start by identifying high-level user activities, such as creating a profile, connecting with friends, and posting content. Each activity is represented as a horizontal row in the user story map.

Breaking down activities into user stories

The team breaks down each activity into smaller user stories that represent specific functionality or interaction points within the platform. For example, under the **Connecting with friends** activity, user stories could include sending friend requests, accepting friend requests, and organizing friends into custom lists.

Prioritizing user stories

Using techniques such as the MoSCoW method or value-based prioritization, the team prioritizes the user stories based on their importance and potential impact on user satisfaction. They identify "must-have" features that are essential for the initial release and consider additional features as "should-have" or "could-have" based on available resources.

Case study – building a task management app

In the context of a case study, let's consider the development of a task management app. The goal of the app is to help individuals and teams organize and track their tasks efficiently. Here are examples of identifying key users and prioritizing features using the "must-have," "should-have," and "could-have" framework.

Identifying key users

Persona 1: Freelancers and solo professionals:

- **Background**: Self-employed individuals who manage their tasks and products
- **Goals**: Streamline task management, improve productivity, and stay organized
- **Pain points**: Difficulty in tracking multiple products, managing deadlines, and prioritizing tasks

Persona 2: Small business teams:

- **Background**: Teams working together on various products and assignments
- **Goals**: Collaborate effectively, delegate tasks, and monitor progress
- **Pain points**: Lack of visibility into team members' tasks, inefficient communication, and product bottlenecks

Persona 3: Product managers:

- **Background**: Professionals responsible for overseeing multiple products and teams
- **Goals**: Monitor product status, allocate resources, and ensure timely delivery
- **Pain points**: Inefficient task assignment, limited product visibility, and difficulty in tracking progress

Prioritizing features

Based on the identified personas, the development team can prioritize features using the "must-have," "should-have," and "could-have" approach.

Must-have features:

- **User account creation and authentication**: Allowing users to create accounts and securely log in to the app

- **Task creation and management**: Enabling users to create, edit, and delete tasks, assign due dates, and set priorities

- **Task filtering and sorting**: Providing options to filter and sort tasks based on different criteria (for example, due date, priority, or assignee)

- **Task notifications**: Sending notifications or reminders to users for upcoming deadlines or task updates

Should-have features:

- **Task comments and discussions**: Enabling users to add comments, discuss tasks, and collaborate with team members

- **Task assignment and delegation**: Allowing users to assign tasks to specific team members and track their progress

- **Task categorization and tags**: Providing options to categorize tasks into different categories or add tags for better organization

- **Integration with calendar and email**: Integrating with external calendar apps or email services to synchronize tasks and deadlines

Could-have features:

- **Task attachments**: Allowing users to attach files or documents to tasks for reference or additional information

- **Task dependencies**: Enabling users to define task dependencies and visualize the relationship between tasks

- **Reporting and analytics**: Providing insights into task completion rates, team performance, and productivity metrics

By categorizing features into "must-have," "should-have," and "could-have," the development team can prioritize their efforts and allocate resources accordingly. This approach ensures that the core functionality required for the initial release is implemented first, while additional features can be considered based on available resources and time constraints.

Case study – collaborative refinement and iterative development

Company X is a software development firm that specializes in creating **customer relationship management** (**CRM**) software for small businesses. They adopted Agile practices to improve their development process and deliver higher-quality products.

Challenge

Company X faced several challenges in their previous development approach. The requirements-gathering process was disconnected from the development team, leading to misunderstandings and misaligned expectations. This resulted in delayed deliveries, rework, and dissatisfied customers. To address these issues, they decided to embrace collaborative refinement and iterative development using user stories.

Approach

Company X formed a cross-functional team consisting of product owners, developers, designers, and quality assurance specialists. They kicked off the product by conducting workshops and meetings to identify the key stakeholders and understand their needs. The team used user story mapping to visualize the product's overall scope and create a shared understanding of the features and their priorities.

They started with a high-level user story map that represented the main functionalities and user flows. The team collaborated to break down these high-level stories into smaller, more manageable user stories that captured specific user interactions and system behaviors. They used the **Independent, Negotiable, Valuable, Estimable, Small, Testable** (**INVEST**) criteria to ensure the quality of the user stories.

Once the user stories were created, the team conducted refinement sessions where they discussed each story in detail. They clarified the acceptance criteria, identified any missing information, and addressed potential technical challenges. During these sessions, the team actively involved the product owners and stakeholders to validate and refine the user stories. This collaborative approach ensured that everyone had a shared understanding of the requirements and minimized the risk of misunderstandings.

The development process followed an iterative approach. The team selected a set of user stories for each iteration based on priority and estimated effort. They worked in short development cycles, typically two weeks, where they developed, tested, and delivered a working increment of the software. At the end of each iteration, they conducted a review meeting with stakeholders to demonstrate the progress and gather feedback.

Results

By adopting collaborative refinement and iterative development using user stories, Company X experienced significant improvements in their development process:

- **Increased stakeholder engagement**: The collaborative approach allowed stakeholders to actively participate in the refinement process, resulting in a shared understanding of the product's features and priorities.

- **Improved alignment**: By breaking down user stories and refining them iteratively, the team achieved better alignment between stakeholders, product owners, and the development team. This reduced misunderstandings and rework.

- **Faster feedback loops**: The iterative development approach enabled frequent feedback from stakeholders, which allowed the team to incorporate changes and adapt the product accordingly.

- **Delivery of value**: The focus on delivering working increments of the software allowed Company X to provide value to customers earlier and gather insights for further improvements.

Overall, the adoption of collaborative refinement and iterative development using user stories transformed Company X's development process. They achieved better collaboration, improved requirements understanding, and delivered high-quality software that met customer needs more effectively.

Case study – validating user stories

Company Y is a mobile app development start-up that aims to create innovative solutions for the fitness industry. They believe in the importance of validating user stories to ensure that their app meets the needs and expectations of their target audience.

Challenge

Company Y faced the challenge of building a fitness-tracking app that would stand out in a crowded market. To overcome this challenge, they recognized the need to validate their user stories and make data-driven decisions during the development process.

Approach

To validate their user stories, Company Y adopted a user-centric approach and employed various techniques throughout the development life cycle. They conducted user research and gathered feedback from potential users, which helped them refine their initial set of user stories.

The team started by identifying their target audience: fitness enthusiasts who wanted a comprehensive app to track their workouts, monitor their progress, and receive personalized recommendations. They conducted interviews, surveys, and usability tests with this target audience to gain insights into their preferences, pain points, and desired features.

Based on the feedback received, Company Y refined their user stories, focusing on the most important and valuable features. They prioritized user stories that aligned with their target audience's needs and goals. They used techniques such as storyboarding and prototyping to visualize the app's user interface and interactions, allowing potential users to provide feedback on the overall user experience.

To validate the user stories further, Company Y conducted beta testing with a group of selected users. They provided access to a test version of the app and encouraged users to explore its features and provide feedback. Through regular communication channels such as surveys, feedback forms, and in-app feedback mechanisms, they collected valuable insights on usability, performance, and missing features.

Results

By diligently validating their user stories, Company Y achieved several positive outcomes:

- **Enhanced user satisfaction**: Validating user stories allowed Company Y to create an app that better met the needs and expectations of their target audience. By incorporating user feedback, they improved the overall user experience and increased user satisfaction.

- **Reduced development risks**: Validating user stories early on helped identify potential issues or gaps in the initial requirements. By addressing these issues promptly, Company Y mitigated risks associated with building features that users did not find valuable or intuitive.

- **Efficient development process**: The validation process enabled Company Y to focus their development efforts on the most critical user stories. By eliminating unnecessary features and incorporating user-driven changes, they optimized their development process and avoided wasting time and resources on less impactful functionalities.

- **Competitive advantage**: Through validation, Company Y was able to differentiate their app from competitors by offering features and experiences that were validated by their target audience. This allowed them to attract more users and gain a competitive edge in the fitness app market.

Overall, the rigorous validation of user stories helped Company Y build an app that resonated with their target audience. By incorporating user feedback and data throughout the development process, they created a successful product that stood out in the competitive fitness industry.

Case study – iterative release and continuous improvement

Company X is a software development company specializing in product management solutions. They believe in the power of iterative release and continuous improvement to deliver value to their customers and stay ahead in the market.

Challenge

Company X faced the challenge of developing a piece of product management software that would cater to the diverse needs of their customers. They wanted to ensure that the software could be released incrementally, allowing them to gather feedback and make improvements based on real-world usage.

Approach

To tackle this challenge, Company X adopted an iterative release and continuous improvement approach. They followed an Agile development methodology and leveraged user stories to capture customer requirements effectively.

The team started by conducting extensive market research and engaging with potential customers to understand their pain points and desired features. They created a backlog of user stories based on this research, focusing on delivering value in each iteration.

In the first release, Company X prioritized the most critical and must-have features identified through user stories. They developed a **minimum viable product** (**MVP**) that addressed the core needs of their target audience. This allowed them to gather feedback from early adopters and validate their assumptions.

After the initial release, Company X closely monitored user feedback, conducting surveys, interviews, and usability tests to gather insights. They used these insights to refine and enhance their user stories for subsequent releases. This feedback helped them identify usability issues, missing features, and areas for improvement.

With each iteration, Company X introduced new features and improvements based on the feedback received. They prioritized user stories that addressed the most pressing needs and pain points of their customers. By releasing frequent updates, they ensured that the software remained relevant and aligned with evolving customer requirements.

Company X also established a feedback loop with their customers, providing channels for users to share their suggestions and report issues. They actively listened to their customers' feedback, acknowledging their input and incorporating valuable suggestions into future releases.

Results

By embracing iterative release and continuous improvement, Company X achieved several positive outcomes:

- **A customer-centric product**: Through iterative releases, Company X developed a product management software that directly addressed the needs and preferences of their customers. They incorporated user feedback and data to shape the product roadmap, resulting in a solution that resonated with their target audience.

- **Rapid value delivery**: By prioritizing and delivering user stories in iterations, Company X was able to provide value to their customers quickly. Early releases allowed them to gather feedback, validate assumptions, and make course corrections, ensuring that each subsequent release delivered incremental value.

- **Enhanced user experience**: Continuous improvement based on user feedback enabled Company X to refine the software's usability, performance, and feature set. They eliminated pain points, introduced intuitive interfaces, and added requested functionalities, leading to an improved user experience.

- **Competitive advantage**: By consistently releasing updates and incorporating customer feedback, Company X maintained a competitive edge in the product management software market. Their agile approach allowed them to adapt to changing customer needs and stay ahead of their competitors.

- **Customer loyalty and retention**: The iterative release process demonstrated Company X's commitment to continuous improvement and customer satisfaction. This fostered trust and loyalty among their customer base, leading to higher customer retention rates and positive word-of-mouth referrals.

Overall, Company X's commitment to iterative release and continuous improvement enabled them to deliver a customer-centric product that evolved with user feedback. By leveraging user stories and embracing an Agile mindset, they achieved rapid value delivery, an enhanced user experience, and a competitive advantage in the market.

Case study – estimating user stories for an e-commerce platform

In this case study, we will explore the process of estimating user stories for the development of an e-commerce platform called "ShopEase." The goal of ShopEase is to provide users with a seamless online shopping experience, allowing them to browse products, make purchases, and track orders. We will follow the journey of a development team as they estimate user stories to plan and prioritize the development of ShopEase.

Defining the product scope

The development team collaborates with stakeholders to define the scope of the product and identify the key features and functionality required for ShopEase. This includes creating a product backlog that contains a list of user stories representing the desired features and user interactions.

Understanding user needs

The team conducts user research and gathers insights into the target audience's preferences, behaviors, and pain points. They identify different user personas, such as casual shoppers and frequent buyers, to represent the diverse user base of ShopEase. This understanding of user needs and expectations helps in estimating user stories more effectively.

Story point estimation

The team adopts the story point estimation technique, where each user story is assigned a relative measure of effort or complexity. They establish a baseline user story, known as the reference story, and assign it a specific number of story points. The team then compares other user stories to the reference story and assigns them story points based on their relative complexity.

Factors influencing estimation

During the estimation process, the team takes into account various factors that can influence the effort required for implementing a user story. These factors include the complexity of the user interface, integration requirements with external systems, data volume, and dependencies on other user stories or modules.

Collaboration and consensus

The team holds estimation meetings where they discuss and collectively estimate each user story. They engage in discussions to clarify requirements, identify potential challenges, and align their understanding of the user story. Through collaboration and consensus, the team reaches a shared understanding of the effort required for each user story.

Adjusting estimates

As the product progresses and more information becomes available, the team may need to adjust their initial estimates. They take into account new insights, technical constraints, and any changes in requirements to refine the estimated effort for each user story. This iterative process ensures that the estimates remain accurate and aligned with the evolving product dynamics.

By monitoring lead time and cycle time, the team gains valuable insights into their delivery process. They can identify areas where work gets delayed or stuck, take actions to improve efficiency, and optimize their workflow. This helps in the effective planning and prioritization of user stories, ensuring that the team can deliver value to the customers promptly.

Continuous improvement

Throughout the product, the team reflects on their estimation accuracy and identifies areas for improvement. They analyze the gaps between the estimated and actual effort to learn from past experiences and refine their estimation practices. This continuous improvement ensures that future estimations become more accurate and reliable.

By effectively estimating user stories, the development team can successfully plan and prioritize the development of ShopEase, an e-commerce platform that meets the needs of its users. Through collaboration, story point estimation, and continuous improvement, the team can gain a better understanding of the effort required for each user story and can allocate resources accordingly. Accurate estimation facilitates effective iteration planning, enhances product transparency, and helps in delivering a high-quality e-commerce platform that provides an exceptional shopping experience for users.

Case study – splitting and refining user stories for a task management application

In this case study, we will explore the process of splitting and refining user stories for the development of a task management application called **TaskTracker**. The goal of TaskTracker is to provide users with a platform to manage and track their tasks efficiently. We will follow the journey of a development team as they split and refine user stories to create well-defined and manageable units of work.

Defining the initial user stories

The development team collaborates with stakeholders to identify the key features and functionalities required for TaskTracker. They create initial user stories that represent the primary user interactions, such as creating tasks, assigning due dates, and marking tasks as complete. These initial user stories serve as the starting point for further refinement.

The development team engages in collaborative discussions with stakeholders, including product owners, users, and other relevant parties, to gather requirements and identify the key features and functionalities needed for the TaskTracker application. Through these interactions, they gain insights into the users' needs, pain points, and desired outcomes.

Based on the information gathered, the team translates the requirements into initial user stories that capture the essential user interactions with the TaskTracker application. These user stories typically represent high-level functionalities, such as creating tasks, assigning due dates, and marking tasks as complete. They serve as the starting point for further refinement and iteration.

During this process, the team ensures that the initial user stories align with the product vision and goals. They focus on understanding the user perspective, considering factors such as user roles, goals, and desired outcomes. By empathizing with the users, the team gains a deeper understanding of their motivations, expectations, and pain points, which helps in crafting user stories that address their specific needs.

Refining user stories

Once the initial user stories have been defined, the team engages in continuous refinement. They collaborate with stakeholders to clarify the requirements, break down larger user stories into smaller, more manageable ones, and add more detailed acceptance criteria.

During the refinement process, the team also considers the technical feasibility and constraints. They assess the effort required to implement each user story and ensure that they are appropriately sized for development and delivery.

Refinement sessions often involve discussions, brainstorming, and feedback loops between the development team and stakeholders. The team iterates on the user stories, adjusting and incorporating changes based on the evolving understanding of the requirements.

By refining user stories, the team ensures that they are well-defined, granular, and aligned with the users' needs. This helps in effectively planning and prioritizing the development efforts, enhancing collaboration and communication within the team, and delivering a high-quality product that meets the users' expectations.

Understanding user needs

The team conducts user research, interviews, and usability tests to gain insights into the target users' needs, preferences, and pain points when managing tasks. This understanding helps the team align user stories with user expectations and ensure they deliver value.

Analyzing and splitting user stories

The team analyzes the initial user stories and identifies opportunities for splitting them into smaller, more manageable units of work. They consider different dimensions for splitting, such as separating user interface components, breaking down complex functionality into simpler steps, or dividing stories based on user roles or system modules.

Refining user stories

Once the user stories have been split, the team focuses on refining them to ensure clarity and specificity. They collaborate with stakeholders, including product owners and users, to clarify requirements, discuss edge cases, and define acceptance criteria. The team ensures that each refined user story captures a specific functionality or user interaction and can be implemented independently.

Estimating effort for refined user stories

The team estimates the effort required for each refined user story using techniques such as story points or ideal days. They consider factors such as complexity, technical dependencies, and the expertise of the team members. Estimation helps the team plan iterations and allocate resources effectively.

Prioritizing and sequencing user stories

Based on the estimated effort and stakeholder priorities, the team prioritizes the refined user stories. They consider factors such as business value, user impact, and dependencies between stories. This prioritization guides the development team in determining the sequence in which user stories will be implemented.

Collaboration and feedback

Throughout the splitting and refining process, the team engages in regular collaboration and seeks feedback from stakeholders. They conduct refinement meetings, demos, and reviews to ensure that the refined user stories meet the stakeholders' expectations and align with the overall vision of TaskTracker.

Iterative development and continuous refinement

The team iteratively develops and delivers increments of functionality based on the refined user stories. During each iteration, they continuously review and refine the user stories to incorporate user feedback, adjust requirements, and adapt to changing product needs. This iterative approach ensures that the user stories remain relevant and aligned with the evolving product vision.

By splitting and refining user stories, the development team can successfully break down the functionality of TaskTracker into well-defined, manageable units of work. This process enables effective planning, estimation, and prioritization, leading to the development of a task management application that meets the needs of its users. Through collaboration, iterative development, and continuous refinement, the team can ensure that the refined user stories capture the essence of the desired functionality and contribute to the overall success of TaskTracker.

Case study – defining acceptance criteria and the definition of done for an e-commerce website

In this case study, we will explore the process of defining acceptance criteria and the **definition of done** (**DoD**) for the development of an e-commerce website called "ShopNow." The objective of ShopNow is to provide users with a seamless online shopping experience. We will follow a development team as they establish clear acceptance criteria and the DoD to ensure the quality and completeness of each user story.

Understanding user requirements

The development team collaborates with stakeholders to understand the requirements of ShopNow. They conduct user interviews, gather feedback, and analyze user expectations to ensure the acceptance criteria align with user needs.

To ensure that the ShopNow application meets the needs of its users, the development team engages in a collaborative process with stakeholders to understand their requirements. This involves conducting user interviews, gathering feedback, and analyzing user expectations.

During user interviews, the team directly interacts with the target users of the application. They ask relevant questions, listen attentively, and observe user behavior to gain valuable insights into their needs, pain points, and preferences. This helps the team understand the context in which the application will be used and identify the key features and functionalities that will address the users' requirements.

In addition to user interviews, the team also gathers feedback from other stakeholders, such as product owners, business analysts, and customer support representatives. This broadens their understanding of the requirements by considering multiple perspectives and ensures that all relevant aspects are taken into account.

To ensure that the acceptance criteria align with the users' needs, the team analyzes the gathered information and synthesizes it into clear and actionable requirements. They identify common patterns, pain points, and desired outcomes to establish a comprehensive understanding of what the application needs to deliver.

Throughout this process, the team emphasizes empathy and user-centered design principles. They put themselves in the users' shoes, seeking to understand their motivations, goals, and challenges. This helps in ensuring that the acceptance criteria capture the essence of what the users are looking for and reflect their expectations.

By actively involving stakeholders, conducting user interviews, gathering feedback, and analyzing user expectations, the development team can ensure that the user requirements for ShopNow are well understood and effectively translated into the acceptance criteria. This lays a strong foundation for the development process and enhances the likelihood of delivering a successful and user-centric product.

Creating user stories

Based on the identified requirements, the team creates user stories that represent the different features and functionalities of ShopNow. Each user story captures a specific user interaction, such as searching for products, adding items to the cart, or making a payment.

Defining acceptance criteria

For each user story, the team collaboratively defines acceptance criteria. These criteria outline the specific conditions that must be met for the user story to be considered complete and ready for release. Acceptance criteria typically include functionality, performance, usability, and security requirements.

Incorporating user perspective

To ensure the acceptance criteria reflect user expectations, the team involves end users in the validation process. They conduct usability testing sessions and gather user feedback to refine the acceptance criteria and ensure they align with the user's perspective.

Establishing the definition of done

In addition to acceptance criteria, the team establishes a clear DoD. The DoD outlines the standards and criteria that must be met for each user story to be considered complete. It includes technical aspects such as code review, unit testing, integration testing, and documentation.

Collaboration and alignment

The development team collaborates with stakeholders, including product owners and quality assurance professionals, to ensure that the acceptance criteria and DoD are well understood and agreed upon. Regular refinement meetings and feedback loops help in clarifying requirements and refining the acceptance criteria.

Continuous improvement

Throughout the development process, the team continuously reviews and refines the acceptance criteria and DoD. They learn from user feedback, conduct retrospectives, and incorporate lessons learned into future iterations. This iterative approach allows for continuous improvement and ensures that the acceptance criteria and DoD remain relevant and effective.

Validation and release

During the development cycle, the team rigorously validates each user story against the defined acceptance criteria and DoD. Once a user story meets all the criteria and fulfills the DoD, it is considered ready for release. This ensures that only high-quality and fully functional features are delivered to end users.

By defining clear acceptance criteria and establishing a robust DoD, the development team can ensure that each user story in the ShopNow e-commerce website meets the required standards and aligns with user expectations. Through collaboration, continuous improvement, and thorough validation, the team can maintain a high level of quality and completeness in the delivered features. The well-defined acceptance criteria and DoD serve as guiding principles for the development team, enabling them to create an exceptional online shopping experience for ShopNow users.

Real-world examples of effective user stories

To further illustrate the concept of effective user stories, let's dive into some real-world examples. These examples will showcase how user stories can be crafted to effectively capture user needs, provide clarity to the development team, and deliver value to the end users. By studying these examples, you'll gain insights into the structure, format, and content of well-written user stories.

Example 1 – online shopping platform

As an online shopper, I want to be able to filter search results by price range so that I can easily find products within my budget. In terms of the acceptance criteria, the search results page should include a filter option where users can input minimum and maximum price values. Upon applying the filter, the search results should update to display products that fall within the specified price range.

This user story focuses on the need of online shoppers to easily find products within their desired price range. The acceptance criteria provide specific details on how the feature should function, ensuring clear expectations for the development team.

Example 2 – task management app

As a product manager, I want to assign tasks to team members so that we can efficiently track progress and collaborate on product deliverables. In terms of the acceptance criteria, the task assignment feature should allow the product manager to select team members from a drop-down list and assign specific tasks to them. Once assigned, team members should receive notifications and be able to update the status of their assigned tasks.

In this user story, the product manager's need to assign tasks and track progress is addressed. The acceptance criteria outline the required functionality of the task assignment feature, ensuring that the development team understands the desired outcome.

Example 3 – a social media platform

As a user, I want the ability to schedule posts for future publishing so that I can plan and manage my social media content in advance. In terms of the acceptance criteria, the scheduling feature should allow users to select a date and time for their post to be published. Scheduled posts should be stored in a queue and automatically published at the specified time.

This user story caters to the needs of social media users who want to streamline their content management. The acceptance criteria outline the specific behavior of the scheduling feature, ensuring that users can plan their posts and have them automatically published at the desired time.

These examples demonstrate how user stories can be concise, focused, and specific, addressing the needs and goals of different user roles. The acceptance criteria provide clear guidelines for the development team, ensuring that the desired functionality is delivered. By studying and analyzing real-world examples, you can gain inspiration and insights for creating effective user stories in your products.

Lessons learned from successful user story implementation

Implementing user stories effectively requires a thoughtful approach and continuous improvement. By examining the experiences of successful user story implementations, we can gain valuable insights and learn important lessons that can guide us in our products. Here are some key lessons learned from successful user story implementation:

- **Collaborative approach**: Successful user story implementation relies on collaboration between the development team, product owners, and stakeholders. By involving all relevant parties in the process, including users and subject matter experts, a more comprehensive and accurate understanding of user needs can be achieved.

- **Clear and concise language**: User stories should be written in clear and concise language, using terminology that is easily understood by all team members. Avoiding technical jargon and focusing on user needs helps foster a shared understanding among the team and reduces the risk of misinterpretation.

- **Iterative refinement**: User stories should be refined and improved over time. Through continuous iteration and feedback from stakeholders, user stories can be adjusted and enhanced to better align with the evolving needs of the product. Regular refinement sessions allow for ongoing improvements and ensure that user stories remain relevant and effective.

- **Regular communication**: Effective communication is crucial in user story implementation. Regularly scheduled meetings, such as daily stand-ups and sprint reviews, provide opportunities for the team to discuss and clarify user stories. Clear communication channels help address any questions or concerns, ensuring that the team remains aligned on the goals and expectations.

- **Validation and feedback**: User stories should be validated and tested with users to ensure they meet their intended purpose. Feedback from users helps refine and improve the user stories, resulting in a better understanding of user needs and more accurate implementation.

- **Adaptability and flexibility**: Agile development embraces adaptability and flexibility. Successful user story implementation requires the team to be open to change and willing to adjust user stories based on new insights and evolving requirements. The ability to adapt and pivot is essential to deliver value to the end users effectively.

By incorporating these lessons into your user story implementation process, you can enhance the effectiveness and impact of user stories in your products. Learning from successful implementations helps you avoid common pitfalls and maximizes the value that user stories can bring to the development process.

Best practices for scaling user stories across teams and products

Scaling user stories across multiple teams and products requires careful planning and coordination to ensure a cohesive and efficient development process. Here are some best practices to consider when scaling user stories:

- **Establish clear guidelines**: Define clear guidelines and standards for creating and formatting user stories across teams and products. This ensures consistency and facilitates easier collaboration and understanding among team members.

- **Maintain a centralized product backlog**: Maintain a centralized product backlog that serves as a single source of truth for user stories. This allows teams to prioritize and work on the most important and valuable features while avoiding duplication of effort.

- **Define cross-team dependencies**: Identify and manage cross-team dependencies to ensure smooth coordination and integration. Clearly communicate dependencies and establish mechanisms for resolving conflicts or aligning priorities across teams.

- **Foster collaboration and communication**: Encourage regular communication and collaboration between teams to ensure alignment on product goals, shared understanding of user needs, and coordination of efforts. This can be facilitated through daily stand-up meetings, regular sync-ups, and cross-team workshops.

- **Utilize Agile scaling frameworks**: Consider implementing agile scaling frameworks such as Scrum of Scrums, Nexus, **Large Scale Scrum** (**LeSS**), or the Spotify model to facilitate coordination and alignment across multiple teams. These frameworks provide guidelines and practices for scaling Agile development while maintaining flexibility and agility.

- **Conduct regular sync-ups**: Schedule regular sync-up meetings or workshops where representatives from different teams can come together to discuss dependencies, align priorities, and share progress. These meetings help identify and address any challenges or bottlenecks early on, fostering collaboration and collective problem-solving.

- **Leverage tools for collaboration**: Utilize collaboration tools and software platforms that enable seamless communication, information sharing, and visibility across teams. These tools can include product management software, communication platforms, and version control systems.

- **Encourage knowledge sharing**: Foster a culture of knowledge sharing and learning across teams. Encourage team members to share best practices, lessons learned, and success stories related to user story implementation. This promotes continuous improvement and allows teams to benefit from each other's experiences.

- **Regularly review and adapt**: Continuously review and adapt your approach to scaling user stories based on feedback and lessons learned. Regular retrospectives and feedback sessions provide valuable insights that can be used to refine and optimize the process.

By following these best practices, you can effectively scale user stories across teams and products, ensuring efficient collaboration, streamlined development, and the successful delivery of valuable software products.

The 3 Cs – Card, Conversation, and Confirmation

The 3 Cs is a concept that helps guide the creation and understanding of user stories. It emphasizes the importance of clarity, collaboration, and confirmation throughout the user story development process. Let's take a closer look at each of the 3 Cs:

- **Card**: The "Card" component refers to the physical or digital representation of the user story. It typically consists of a short description written on a notecard or in a user story management tool. The card provides a concise and clear summary of the user story, capturing the essence of what the user wants to achieve and why.

  The card should include essential information such as the user persona, the desired action or functionality, and the expected outcome or benefit. It should be written in a way that is easy to understand and communicates the user's perspective effectively.

- **Conversation**: The "Conversation" component of the 3 Cs emphasizes the importance of ongoing dialogue and collaboration between the product owner, development team, and stakeholders. User stories are not meant to be rigid specifications but rather serve as conversation starters to foster a deeper understanding of user needs and requirements.

  Engaging in conversations around user stories allows for clarification, exploration of different perspectives, and identification of potential challenges or opportunities. It helps ensure that everyone involved has a shared understanding of the user story and can contribute their insights and expertise.

- **Confirmation**: The "Confirmation" aspect of the 3 Cs focuses on defining and agreeing upon the acceptance criteria for the user story. Acceptance criteria outline the specific conditions or requirements that must be met for the user story to be considered complete and acceptable.

  During the confirmation stage, the product owner and development team work together to define measurable and testable criteria that demonstrate the successful implementation of the user story. These criteria serve as objective benchmarks for confirming that the story has been implemented to meet the user's needs and expectations.

The 3 Cs framework encourages collaboration, clarity, and alignment throughout the user story development process. By leveraging the power of clear and concise cards, engaging in meaningful conversations, and establishing agreed-upon acceptance criteria, teams can effectively capture and deliver user value in an agile and collaborative manner.

Agile product requirements documents

In Agile development, the traditional approach of creating extensive and detailed **product requirements documents** (**PRDs**) is often replaced with a more iterative and flexible approach. However, there are instances where having a well-crafted **Agile product requirements document** (**APRD**) can be beneficial. Let's explore the key aspects of Agile PRDs:

- **The purpose of Agile PRDs**: Agile PRDs serve as a reference and communication tool to capture and communicate product requirements and vision. While they may not have the same level of detail as traditional PRDs, they provide a high-level overview of the product's objectives, features, and user needs. Agile PRDs focus on the "why" and "what" aspects of the product rather than the detailed "how."

- **Key components**: Agile PRDs typically include the following components:

  - **Product vision**: A concise statement that outlines the overall purpose and goals of the product.

  - **User personas**: Profiles of the target users, including their characteristics, needs, and goals.

  - **User stories**: Brief descriptions of specific user interactions or scenarios, highlighting the user's goal, action, and expected outcome.

  - **Feature prioritization**: A prioritized list of features based on their value, impact, and alignment with the product vision.

  - **Acceptance criteria**: Clear and measurable criteria that define when a feature is considered complete and meets user expectations.

  - **Constraints and assumptions**: Any known limitations, dependencies, or assumptions that may impact the development and delivery of the product.

- **Flexibility and iteration**: Agile PRDs embrace the Agile principle of being adaptable and open to change. They are not set in stone but rather evolve and iterate as the product progresses. The focus is on maintaining a living document that can be updated and refined based on continuous feedback, learning, and evolving user needs.

- **Collaboration and communication**: Agile PRDs are meant to foster collaboration and ensure a shared understanding among all stakeholders. They serve as a reference point for discussions, decision-making, and aligning the team's efforts. Regular communication and feedback loops are essential to ensure that the PRD remains relevant and up to date.

- **Balancing documentation and agility**: Agile PRDs strike a balance between providing enough information to guide development and allowing for flexibility and adaptation. They should be concise, easily accessible, and updated regularly to reflect the evolving nature of the product.

Agile PRDs can be valuable tools for aligning stakeholders, providing clarity, and guiding the development of Agile products. While they may not be as extensive as traditional PRDs, they serve as a dynamic reference point that captures the essential aspects of the product and facilitates collaboration and effective decision-making throughout the development process.

Summary

Throughout this chapter, we explored various case studies that showcased real-world examples of applying user stories in practice. These case studies provided valuable insights into the practical implementation of user stories and highlighted their effectiveness in Agile development.

In the case study on creating effective user stories, we followed the journey of a product team developing a new mobile application. By leveraging user-centered design principles and conducting user research, they were able to craft compelling user stories that captured the needs and goals of their target audience. Through clear and concise language, the team effectively communicated their requirements and laid the foundation for a successful product.

The case study on user story mapping demonstrated the power of visualizing user stories and their relationships. We witnessed a team working on a complex e-commerce platform using story mapping to identify dependencies, prioritize features, and create a roadmap for development. By breaking down the user stories into smaller, actionable tasks and mapping them across different stages of the user journey, the team gained a holistic view of the product and improved collaboration and alignment.

In the case study on estimating user stories, we followed an Agile development team as they tackled the challenge of estimating the effort and complexity of their backlog. Through techniques such as story points and relative estimation, the team gained a better understanding of the size and effort required for each user story. This allowed them to plan their iterations more effectively, manage stakeholders' expectations, and deliver value predictably.

Lastly, the case study on acceptance criteria and the DoD emphasized the importance of clear and measurable criteria for successful implementation. We observed a team refining their user stories by collaboratively defining acceptance criteria and establishing the DoD. This ensured a shared understanding of the expected outcomes and facilitated effective communication between the development team and stakeholders. Finally, we covered best practices, the 3Cs, and Agile product documents.

By studying these case studies, you have gained practical insights into the application of user stories across different scenarios and industries. You learned how to create effective user stories, refine them through story mapping, estimate effort, and define acceptance criteria. Armed with these practical examples, you are now equipped to apply these strategies and techniques to your agile development products, leading to improved collaboration, enhanced product outcomes, and greater stakeholder satisfaction.

In the next chapter, we will dive into the realm of expert interviews, exploring how gathering insights from industry experts can further enhance the understanding of user needs and inform the creation of effective user stories.

Questions

Answer the following questions to test your knowledge of this chapter:

1. What common challenges are faced when implementing user stories in practice?
2. How can user story mapping help in product planning?
3. What are some best practices for estimating user stories?
4. How can acceptance criteria and the DoD enhance the quality of user stories?
5. How can user stories contribute to effective collaboration between the development team and stakeholders?

Answers

Here are the answers to this chapter's questions:

1. Implementing user stories can come with its own set of challenges. Some common ones include difficulty in defining clear acceptance criteria, estimating effort accurately, handling dependencies between user stories, and ensuring effective collaboration between the development team and stakeholders.
2. User story mapping is a valuable technique for product planning. It helps teams visualize the user journey and identify the flow of user stories. By breaking down user stories into smaller tasks and arranging them in a logical sequence, teams can prioritize features, identify dependencies, and create a roadmap for development.

3. Estimating user stories can be challenging but there are some best practices to consider. Using techniques such as story points or relative estimation, involving the entire team in estimation discussions, and using historical data or benchmarks for reference can improve the accuracy of estimates. Regularly reviewing and refining estimates based on actual team velocity and feedback from previous iterations is also recommended.

4. Clear acceptance criteria and a well-defined DoD are essential for the successful implementation of user stories. Acceptance criteria help define the expected outcomes and ensure that the team and stakeholders have a shared understanding of what constitutes a complete and satisfactory implementation. The DoD sets the quality standards and criteria that must be met before a user story is considered complete. Both of these elements enhance the quality and clarity of user stories, resulting in improved product outcomes.

5. User stories provide a common language and understanding between the development team and stakeholders. By expressing requirements from the perspective of the end user, user stories facilitate effective communication, help align expectations, and encourage collaboration. They enable the team and stakeholders to focus on delivering value to the user and foster a shared sense of ownership and responsibility for the product's success.

8
Expert Interviews

Welcome to this chapter of expert interviews on user stories! In this unique chapter, we have the privilege of delving into insightful conversations with industry experts who possess extensive experience and knowledge in the realm of user stories. Through these interviews, you will have the opportunity to gain valuable insights, expert opinions, and practical advice from leaders in the field of Agile development and user story practices.

Through these interviews, we will explore a wide range of user story-related topics, providing you with a diverse and comprehensive understanding of expert insights. Get ready to dive into these thought-provoking interviews with esteemed experts in the field of user stories and gain a wealth of knowledge that will empower you to elevate your Agile development practices and deliver exceptional products to your users!

In this chapter, we're going to delve into conversations with the following experts:

- Expert 1 – Sean Mack
- Expert 2 – Bob Galen
- Expert 3 – Michael Spayd
- Expert 4 – Lyssa Adkins

By the end of this chapter, you will have an understanding of some expert perspectives on user stories and the practical guidance they provide. You will have gained valuable insights into industry trends, advanced techniques, and innovative approaches to optimizing your user story practices.

Expert 1 – Sean Mack

Our first expert, Sean Mack, is a CIO.com CIO100 award recipient. He is a visionary technology executive with extensive experience in cybersecurity, development, DevOps, platform engineering, program management, and architecture. He is an innovative leader driving global business strategy and transformation. Sean manages large, globally distributed teams with significant direct budget responsibility. Let's begin!

Can you tell us about your role as the CIO at Wiley and how it related to user stories?

More and more, the role of the CIO focuses on innovation and transformation. We are no longer just keeping things running; we are also building new products and new ways of working. This is where user stories come in. At Wiley, we would have many innovative projects running at any one time, from deployment automation to end user workflow automation, and each of these was managed using Agile delivery methodologies.

How did you ensure that the user stories you implemented aligned with the business objectives of Wiley?

The linkage between business objectives and user stories goes all the way back to annual planning. At the beginning of the year, we would map out our objectives and measures. Based on this, we would map out the work we wanted to do to accomplish these objectives. The work would then be broken down into program increments that we would deliver against using Agile and user stories. In this way, there would be a line all the way from the original user story to our overarching business objectives.

How did you measure the success of the user stories that were implemented at Wiley? What metrics did you use to evaluate their impact?

We used several metrics to evaluate progress and the impact of user stories. At Wiley, we implemented flow metrics, which gave us some great visibility into the flow of work as well as the type of work that was getting done. In addition, on a quarterly basis, we measured how we were progressing against our business objectives. Because there was a link between the work we were doing on a daily basis and our business objectives, we were able to see the impact our work was having.

Expert 2 – Bob Galen

Bob Galen is an Agile leader, coach, author, speaker, and community builder. He has a knack for turning around struggling organizations, teams, and products in a sustainable and productive way. Bob is also a proven team builder and a servant-leader. For 20 years, he has been focusing on leveraging Agile methods as the best way to deliver software value. While not being a silver bullet, they simply work better than anything Bob has tried.

Can you tell us about your role as director of Agile practices at Zenergy Technologies, and how it relates to user stories?

I'm not sure there's a direct relationship. My role at Zenergy is that of an Agile consultant: I'm an Agile coach, a trainer, and a transformation artist helping organizations transform to Agile ways of working. I've been doing that for more than 20 years. User stories are an area within that. One of the areas of passion I've had historically is product ownership – I've written a book on it. I worked on the first edition of that book in 2009. One of the earliest requirements artifacts from extreme programming was the notion of the user story.

Between the late 1990s and early 2000s, I was leading teams and being part of teams that were building software. We were articulate, moving from big requirements documents to user stories and trying to figure out what good user stories look like and whenever appropriate, having this discussion at Zenergy, with the client. Often, clients need help grasping what a container is ("What does a good one look like?") and how to construct them ("What is the process for evolving and refining them?"). So, I think of backlog refinement as being part of the genesis of user stories. I muck around with user stories fairly frequently with clients and try to help them with that.

In your experience, what are some challenges teams usually face when creating user stories, and how can they overcome them?

The biggest anti-pattern that I've seen for new teams is *writing less*. You've probably seen this as well. Everyone has their own fundamental opinion on how to handle requirements in a Waterfall model. Both the bad news and the good news is the training. There is also the rigor that organizations put into having traditional requirements specifications and training people to write lengthy descriptions of physical requirements and UX. The traditional requirements were in volumes, and they did a great job of writing them.

As a coach, I get blank stares when I'm trying to teach people what a user story is because they think they need to have all that information; they think they can't build without incredibly detailed requirement information. They think they need everything defined upfront. But that's not the nature of the user story. So, that's a hurdle for people, and it's incredibly uncomfortable.

You should write less at the beginning. Whoever is writing the user story should write just a placeholder. Folks get really uncomfortable with that. I'll say, "Just write a headline and a couple of notes for yourself. That's it." They'll reply, "What about acceptance criteria?" I say, "Leave the acceptance criteria. It's a note. Flesh it out over time." Instead of trying to write it all upfront, write something very terse and incomplete. The essence of the user story is to have a lot of ambiguity built in. It's not intended to be completed in the beginning – teams are uncomfortable with that.

User stories are intended to be a complete definition at the end of the sprint. There's a curve associated with building user story completeness. I've used different percentages over time. I'll tell teams, "You only need a user story to be 30% or 40% complete by the time it enters a sprint." There's nothing magic about that number. But what I'm trying to say is that it's a terse artifact to begin with. You only have to define the key bits in order to get a picture of what you're implementing, estimate it, and de-risk it before you start executing it. That's a very different paradigm for teams and it takes time to make it work.

So, what I say is, write a bad user story. Just force yourself to write less. Everyone's going to be uncomfortable, and the team is going to yell at the product owner. We can provide an initial estimate for a user story even when complete information isn't available. Embrace the uncertainty or evolving requirements, letting details naturally unfold as time progresses.

I'm a bit of an adjuster. Sometimes, I'll write a user story that's actually nonsensical. What I'm trying to do is to get the team to call me out on it. I want them to say, "This is absurd," so I can reply, "Okay, I'm sorry. Who can write it better than I just did?" It's good to have that collaborative definition. In most teams, someone responds and contributes, and it pulls the team together. There are some facilitation tricks you can use, such as the one I just mentioned, to pull people in: teams want an individual to own it and to tell them what to do. That's a traditional requirement. But user stories try to create more collaborative solutions.

Can you share any examples of how user stories have significantly impacted the success of a project?

I don't want order-takers on the team. I want collaborators. I want everyone to be a chef. I want projects where the team takes full ownership rather than just implementing stuff.

Projects don't need to be perfectly agile in order to succeed. Instead, independent problem-solving and initiative are expected. I can't tell you how many times we've finished a project and the customer said, "That's not what I wanted." You've seen that and heard that. My genesis is in Waterfall. We laid off hundreds of people when we blew up projects. So, the idea of having small requirements in bite-sized chunks, emergent understanding, and collaborating teams sounds fluffy, but it also leads to good results, and the customer is part of that.

I remember Extreme Programming teams, which were the genesis of user stories in XP. There wasn't a product owner – typically, the Product Owner was **Business Analyst (BA)** writing stories, but the customer was right there. We would collaborate on the stories whenever we needed to. We had much more successful outcomes.

Now, the challenge is doing them well, not perfectly. It's a balancing act. For example, how many stories are you writing ahead? Organizations can make the mistake of writing all the stories in advance. How much "look ahead" are you doing iteratively? Because you're going to make discoveries, and that's going to affect your story definition later on.

So, if I get that balance right with teams, the outcomes are usually much better – maybe not a phenomenal success, but much better relative to their historical execution.

How do you ensure that the user stories you implemented aligned with the business objectives of Zenergy Technologies?

One of the core mistakes made historically was that, traditionally, requirements were abstracted from the client. Someone else was interpreting the user or the client, transmogrifying those things into documents, and handing them off to the team. Teams very rarely saw the requester, so there was a communication gap that naturally occurred. So, at Zenergy or any other company, how do we ensure that we're doing the right thing?

You get the customers engaged with the team: not just at sprint reviews, but during backlog, refinement, and whenever appropriate. We could be talking business stakeholders or UX stakeholders. The broader you can be, the better. There could be user stories that have architectural implications: in that case, you want to make sure that you're including architects in your discussions. You don't want to have meetings for meetings' sake but ensure that the appropriate people are there and that they're co-creating the story.

There's this notion of something called the Three Amigos. The metaphor may be poorly received nowadays, but the point is about getting different perspectives involved in the creation and emergence of a user story. The basic idea of the Three Amigos of software development is that these "amigos" typically consist of representatives from development, testing or QA, and product management. They collaborate closely to define and refine software requirements. However, depending on the type of story, you could also have an "amigo" from the architecture or DevOps team. These "amigos" don't just write the requirements; they shape them together in a collaborative manner. They are there as guides through the system. The "amigos" aren't just a writing authority; they are shepherds who ensure the delivery of value. So, at Zenergy, we try to make sure that we're getting that connection.

The second thing that I think is important is the acceptance criteria. A lot of companies underuse acceptance criteria and don't prioritize it effectively. Some folks have miscellaneous acceptance criteria. It's just there because the template says it needs to be. Some folks have tons of acceptance criteria, which confuses the value of things. Some folks have too little or nonsensical acceptance criteria. There has to be a balancing act.

One method I use to explain acceptance criteria is geared toward testers. Testers should look at acceptance criteria to get a sense of what's important to the client in order to prioritize their tests.

There's the notion of risk-based testing, where you test the more valuable bits of an app or a function more than the other, less valuable bits. Well, how do you know where the value is? The acceptance criteria, if written with value in mind, will give you hints as to what the product owner and the customer think is valuable. But what are the critical business aspects of the story? You want to make sure that you hammer on them as a tester. You need to test everything.

I want developers to do the same thing with me. There might be critical areas of a piece of software that need to be carefully designed for performance. So, if there's an acceptance criterion related to system performance, it's not just a checkbox but something that is exciting and causes the development team to say, "Oh, this is critical – we had better be thorough in how we think about integrating this in the overall system design." So, the acceptance criteria are really important to delivering value, as long as you invest in them right.

How did you measure the success of the user stories that are implemented at Zenergy Technologies? What metrics did you use to evaluate their impact?

I think metrics are part of an overall program. We don't do a lot with them; we're a consulting firm. In our work with clients, we place a strong emphasis on delivering outcome-based value. That means we're more interested in providing tangible benefits that directly impact our clients and their customer base. Rather than focusing strictly on metrics such as "story completeness," we prioritize value-driven outcomes, demonstrating how our work positively affects the client's objectives. For instance, "How often is the customer delighted?" That's called a teardrop metric.

This is going to sound odd, but you can have negative teardrops, or you can have the highest of teardrops, but what are the teardrops you're getting from clients who were seeing it in a review? Customers are saying, "That's exactly what I was envisioning. In fact, just two days ago in our interim, you all did an excellent job – truly knocked it out of the park." Personally, I believe there are various metrics we can focus on, beyond just the immediate results. We could consider throughput metrics, which measure the amount of work completed over a given period, or even lot-sized-sized metrics (lot-sized metrics refer to measurements of performance or quality that are based on a specific quantity of units, often called a "lot."). These metrics can apply to a variety of contexts, but they are commonly used in manufacturing and supply chain management. In manufacturing, a "lot" is a batch or a set of units that are processed together. Lot-sized metrics can help determine things such as the efficiency of production processes, the quality of products being produced, or the cost per unit of output.

For example, in quality control, a common lot-sized metric is the defect rate, which measures the number of defective units in a given lot. Similarly, in supply chain management, a lot-sized metric could refer to the cost of storing or transporting a specific lot size.

Please note that lot-sizing also refers to a crucial decision in inventory management about how much to order or produce at once. This decision directly impacts holding costs (the costs of keeping items in stock) and ordering or setup costs (the costs associated with placing an order or setting up the production process).

Different lot-sizing techniques (such as economic order quantity, lot-for-lot, or periodic order quantity) aim at balancing these costs and are often part of an inventory management or production planning system, which evaluates the optimal order size for production, among others.

To me, the most important outcome is the value added for the customer. Is it what the customer wanted? Are we delivering earned value? Project managers have this notion of earned value, and that relates to validating the value of the construction of software. I don't think of earned value in a Project Management Institute sense. The "teardrops" represent whether or not we've provided the expected value from the customer's perspective. Essentially, we're asking, "Have we completed the project to their satisfaction? Is our work finished and ready to be put on the shelf?" And most importantly, it's the customer who makes that determination. So, we're very tightly coupled with that, probably because we're more consultative.

Expert 3 – Michael Spayd

Michael Spayd is the founder and chief executive of The Collective Edge. His work can be summed up well by a quote from a client, who said, "If you're not ready for change, don't call Michael." That felt like a real compliment for Michael, and a powerful summary of his life's mission: Michael's purpose is "transformation." This purpose has evolved of late to be specifically "transforming transformers," as he focuses his teaching, systemic healing, and shadow consulting work on growing change agents.

What are your thoughts on the whole philosophical shift from requirements to user stories? Why was that so important, and what was the impact?

Well, I started with user stories back in 2001, and that was really edgy at the time. User stories were perceived as only for small teams and non-mission-critical projects. I've been pondering this quite a bit since our last discussion. There's a significant difference between talking to a customer or a user and talking to a business analyst who may not even be part of the development team. The latter might simply write a requirements document and not be involved in the actual creation of the product.

The analyst will ask the customer to define everything they want in the product, often requiring them to spell it out in exhaustive detail. It's a process that can be overly meticulous and time-consuming.

Users tend to list everything they could possibly want in a product, not just what they truly need. This is because they feel that if they don't express all their desires right away, they might not get another chance to do so later. The user's desires are then incorporated into a requirements document. This process often involves an intermediary, such as a business analyst, who translates the user's needs and wants into formalized requirements. It's not going to be the person who's going to develop it, and they'll never talk with the developer.

Then you have a formal document that you've signed. The requirements document as a contract between you and the development team or the business analysts have been disappointing for the development. That's the old paradigm.

The new paradigm is to say, "Let's have a really informal placeholder. We're going to put it on an index card to show just how ephemeral it is – it's a placeholder for a future conversation." That's what I used to teach people. A user story is a placeholder for a future conversation. It is not, and it doesn't need to be, a detailed requirement. It's just enough to estimate what you'll need. It's a game piece that you use to play the game of Agile. It is fundamental in how the game is played from a formal contract back to a friendly conversation.

Introducing a user story also fundamentally changes the tone of the process. It's not a list of requirements. It is a story about what you envision, what you think would be cool, and what's important to a user. So, it establishes a completely different dynamic. It changes the "game" we're playing, so to speak. It makes it a different kind of venture.

Business analysts essentially tell their customers, "You've got to play the game my way." We're technical people, so we like lots of detail. We start considering various possibilities: "What if this scenario occurs? What if that changes?" The process becomes a cooperative endeavor, more like a friendly conversation than a traditional business interaction. The user story sets the tone for that.

Then you can use it as a placeholder in the planning game. You use it as a marker of the game pieces. Then, when you need to work on it, you pull it down off the wall and have a conversation with a customer who's sitting right there with you, ready to collaborate. Rather than restricting collaboration to specific phases or just the project's initiation, collaboration is an ongoing process that happens daily. I can start with an initial collaborative discussion, then continue developing the project while keeping the conversation alive. This approach turns the process into a constant dialog that accompanies the work progression.

Previously, the requirements process essentially functioned as a semi-formal contract. Once it was signed, it was considered a comprehensive representation of everything required from the project. We completed the requirements process long before we embarked on the implementation phase. The business analyst doesn't know anything about writing code, so they're in no position to judge what's feasible or not. So, it's a serial, ongoing, collaborative game. [The approach to development has shifted from a rigid, linear process to a fluid, iterative, and collaborative process, as embodied by Agile methodologies.]

User stories signal a new way that is a different kind of venture. In the past, we adhered to a different kind of game. As mentioned before, the requirements process was like a semi-formal contract, defining everything we wanted up front. This has changed; we now work differently.

This new approach has implications not only for customers but also for the rest of the team. It simplifies the process, with us transitioning from lengthy written documents to a more visual representation. For instance, consider the shift from a detailed requirements document, which a given developer would only engage with in a limited way, to something like an index card on the wall in the team room.

This index card becomes shared property within the community. Team members can move it around, show it to each other, and engage with it directly. A tester, for instance, can start with it when creating conditions of satisfaction, discussing it with both the developer and the product owner from the very beginning.

This method transforms the process into a more communal and collaborative effort, similar to using a mini whiteboard. Instead of an individual taking a task to their desk and solving it in isolation, problem-solving becomes a shared, spirited discussion. Within a sprint or an iteration, a team member might refer to the card multiple times over several days, rather than just taking a snapshot of it.

This approach encourages ongoing, collaborative problem-solving instead of solitary work.

Expert 4 – Lyssa Adkins

Lyssa Adkins is an Agile and professional coach, facilitator, teacher, and inspirer. Her current focus is on improving the performance of top leadership teams through insightful facilitation and organization systems coaching. Making difficult decisions faster and with clear alignment, unknotting challenging multi-department impediments, creating the conditions for smooth organizational delivery, and helping leaders take up the Agile transformation that is theirs to make…this is where Lyssa thrives and helps others to thrive.

I would be interested in hearing your take on the whole philosophical shift from requirements to user stories, why that was so important, and the impact of user stories.

I think of Agile practices as patterns that interrupt unconscious learned behavior. I have a deep familiarity with project requirements from my 15 years of experience as a project manager and a project management office lead. During this time, I was often responsible for ensuring that we thoroughly understood and nailed down the requirements before engaging a team to start creating.

The traditional process has its shortcomings. With this approach, the team often ends up being spoon-fed requirements. Unfortunately, these requirements often fail to fully meet what the customer needs. In essence, what we deliver can turn out to be not fit for purpose.

With the traditional approach, we assume the client or customer actually understands what they need, especially if we're building something new that nobody's ever seen before. In our desire to have certainty and to predict how things are going to flow, we nail down requirements. But this is doomed to fail. The reality is, you will get minor issues or "edges" that keep surfacing. You try to address them through change requests, but that leads to disputes between the client and the development team. The client argues, assuming certain elements were included in the original agreement, leading to confusion and disagreement. The client says, "You should have known that," and the team replies, "How could we have known that?" There's then a lot of blaming and finger-pointing.

So, that's the legacy we're coming from. In the shift from requirements to user stories, one of the things I love about user stories is the interrupt pattern. I believe it was Phil Wait who said that a user story is a placeholder for a future conversation. It is not meant to be a complete rundown of exactly what needs to be created, because if we're serving the client well, we actually don't know how to create what needs to be created. We need to be in really good conversation with the people who are asking for the thing to figure out the best way to satisfy their current understanding of what they want. We need to give grace on both sides to allow our understanding of both the technology and the business need to change as we learn so that we can actually deliver something that people will use.

So, that's why I view it as an interrupt pattern. It's not that user stories are necessarily the way we're always going to do things. It's just that the formulaic method of them, the lack of detailed specification, serves to interrupt how we think about handing down requirements to a team.

There was once a survey called a **chaos report** that said that 70% of the features that we build are rarely or never used. Part of the reason why is that the customer or client's conception of what they wanted at the beginning came as a result of them drawing up requirements with a mindset of, "I have to get this all down now because I will not have another chance to communicate with the team or change things." I used to say, "Okay, go ahead, throw in the kitchen sink, because you're not going to have a chance to have your input later." I would actually encourage people to do that, in the old way of working. So, it ended up that we would build a bunch of stuff that people never used.

Not only is the user story a promise for future conversation and collaboration, but it also completes the feedback loop with customers so that we can ask them, "Do you care about what we just built? Will you actually use it? If not, how can we change it?" The user story makes things that much more effective.

Even just the idea that the person who wants the thing and the people who are delivering the thing come together to talk frequently is another important aspect. It used to be that our options for technological solutions were limited. The world was just all over the place. Information was not as ubiquitous and customers were not as choosy. In those conditions, the idea of one group sitting down with the customer, eliciting their requirements, and then handing it off to a completely different group to actually implement it was at least more plausible. But in a world where information is ubiquitous, things change quicker, and technological choices proliferate, things need to be a lot more responsive to what's going on than just working with a predictive plan. That's another reason why working with user stories helps us.

The workplace is becoming more human than it used to be, mostly because of the shift from conceiving of organizations as machines that can run to conceiving of organizations as ecosystems that thrive, survive, or die together. We've shifted to a much more realistic view, where we focus on what is actually happening rather than what we're trying to force to happen. As a plan-driven project manager, there were many situations where I found myself pretending that certain things weren't happening when they actually were. The shift toward a more human way of working gives us all a lot of genuine accountability, but also another side of that grace. We don't know what we don't know until we start moving together. And the "we" here are the people who are asking for the thing and the people who are creating whatever that thing is. That goes a long way in a complex world where there are very few black-and-white answers or straightforward strategies that will work for their law.

Is there anything else that you wanted to share regarding user stories?

I haven't thought about user stories in a very long time. I don't necessarily think that user story practices are the be-all-and-end-all, but I treat user story practices in the same way as I do Agile. People come to me and ask, "If I want to change this about the Agile framework I'm working in, is that okay?" I simply say to them, "Look at the values of the Agile framework you're working on. If the thing you want to change is still going to uphold those values, then give it a go." It's a similar thing with user stories: no matter what formats or patterns we create around them, if they uphold what agility is going for, allow us to express those values, and don't detract from our ability to live those values, give it a go. But the most important thing is not to forget the *inspect and adapt* loop. Find out whether it worked; if it didn't, go back. If it did, go forward. All this sounds cut and dry, but the truth is that humans are involved, and each individual human has their own edges and their own places that they're unwilling to go. That's what makes this so beautiful and messy.

Takeaways

I hope these insightful interviews have helped amplify your knowledge. Here are some of the key takeaways from these interviews.

Expert 1 – Sean Mack, CIO at Wiley

- Sean Mack discussed the crucial role of the CIO in fostering innovation and transformation within an organization

- He explained how Wiley leverages user stories to manage their innovative projects effectively

- Mack emphasized the importance of aligning user stories with business objectives to achieve desired outcomes

- He detailed Wiley's annual planning process, which is designed to align user stories with broader business goals

- Lastly, Mack highlighted how Wiley measures project success using flow metrics and by tracking progress against business objectives

Expert 2 – Bob Galen, Agile consultant and coach at Zenergy Technologies

- Bob Galen illustrated the role of an Agile consultant in incorporating user stories into a team's workflow

- He presented user stories as an essential part of the Agile transformation process

- Galen discussed the common challenges teams face when creating user stories and provided strategies to overcome these obstacles

- He stressed the importance of brevity and embracing ambiguity in user stories

- Galen underscored the necessity of customer involvement in creating user stories, advocating for a collaborative approach

- He shared examples of successful projects where user stories were employed effectively

- To ensure user stories align with business objectives, Galen recommended frequent customer engagement and collaboration

- He also addressed the role of acceptance criteria in defining critical aspects of projects and prioritizing tests

- Lastly, Galen suggested measuring success through outcome-based value and customer satisfaction metrics

Expert 3 – Michael Spayd, founder and CEO of The Collective Edge

- Michael Spayd discussed the philosophical shift from traditional requirements to user stories

- He explained the value of using user stories as informal placeholders for future conversations rather than detailed requirements

- Spayd highlighted how user stories set a collaborative and friendly tone for the development process

- He talked about the transformation from a traditional "arm's length" relationship to a conversational and collaborative venture

- He shared how user stories serve as game pieces in the planning process

- Spayd emphasized the importance of daily interaction and collaboration with customers

- He described the transition from a sequential process to a continual and collaborative "game"

- Spayd also stressed the concept of joint ownership and the accessibility of user stories within the team, promoting shared problem-solving through collaborative discussions

Expert 4 – Lyssa Adkins, Agile and professional coach, facilitator, and teacher

- Lyssa Adkins discussed the legacy of "spoon-feeding" requirements that don't truly meet the customer's needs

- She talked about the shift from requirements to user stories as a disruptive pattern that challenges unconscious learning and behavior

- Adkins emphasized user stories as placeholders for future conversations and collaborative understanding

- She advocated for grace and flexibility in the face of evolving understanding and technological changes

- Adkins addressed the need to break from the pattern of detailed specification and to instead promote a collaborative approach

- She highlighted the importance of completing the feedback loop with customers to ensure that features deliver value and are usable

- Adkins underscored the necessity of frequent conversations between the customer and the delivery team

- She recommended a sense-and-respond approach in a world filled with abundant information and advancing technology

- Lastly, Adkins discussed the need for genuine accountability and grace in a complex world and the importance of aligning changes with the underlying values of Agile frameworks

Example scenario

Company X is firmly committed to enhancing its UX by focusing on two pivotal business objectives: increasing user engagement and reducing customer support tickets. Key metrics and flow measures, such as **Monthly Active Users (MAU)**, lead time, cycle time, throughput, and **Work in Progress (WIP)**, are leveraged to gain insightful data. These tracked parameters help in identifying bottlenecks and streamlining development and support processes, thus ensuring faster delivery and efficient issue resolution, and ultimately resulting in superior user engagement and satisfaction.

In a bid to drive higher user engagement, Company X has strategized a meticulous tracking mechanism centered around a key set of metrics. The major metric being observed is **Monthly Active Users (MAU)**, serving as a testament to the reach and acceptance of their platform. To supplement this, the company has turned to flow metrics, namely lead time and cycle time. The lead time is a measure of the time duration from when a user story is first identified to when it is finally deployed. In contrast, cycle time measures the period taken to finish a user story once it's under active development. Scrutinizing these flow metrics enables Company X to thoroughly understand the efficiency of their development processes, allowing for the detection and rectification of potential bottlenecks or inefficiencies. Such vigilance in tracking can reveal an extended lead time or cycle time, highlighting areas needing improvement to expedite delivery, ultimately enhancing user engagement.

Business objective – increase user engagement

- **Metric**: MAU.

- **Flow metrics**: Lead time, cycle time.

- **Tracking**: In addition to tracking the MAU, Company X also measured lead time and cycle time as flow metrics. Lead time represents the time it takes from the identification of a user story to its deployment, while cycle time represents the time it takes for a user story to be completed once actively worked on. By monitoring these flow metrics, Company X can gain insights into the efficiency of their development process and identify areas for improvement. For example, if they notice a high lead time or cycle time, it may indicate bottlenecks or inefficiencies in their development workflow that need to be addressed to ensure faster delivery and better user engagement.

In line with its business objective to minimize customer support tickets, Company X is placing significant emphasis on a strategic set of metrics. The central metric in this pursuit is the volume of customer support tickets, which directly reflects the scale of customer issues. To complement this, the company has incorporated flow metrics into its tracking, namely throughput and **Work In Progress (WIP)**. Throughput signifies the rate at which user stories are accomplished and delivered to customers, and WIP indicates the quantity of user stories that are being actively worked on at any given point in time. By vigilantly monitoring these flow metrics, Company X is better equipped to evaluate the effectiveness of their support ticket resolution process and detect any potential bottlenecks or constraints. This tracking mechanism enables the company to optimize throughput and manage WIP proficiently, thereby facilitating the reduction in the total number of customer support tickets, ultimately contributing to enhanced customer satisfaction.

Business objective – reduce customer support tickets

- **Metric**: Customer support ticket volume.

- **Flow metrics**: Throughput, WIP.

- **Tracking**: In addition to tracking the volume of support tickets, Company X can also leverage flow metrics such as throughput and WIP. Throughput measures the rate at which user stories are completed and delivered to customers, while WIP represents the number of user stories actively being worked on at any given time. By monitoring these flow metrics, Company X can assess the efficiency of their support ticket resolution process and identify any bottlenecks or constraints that may be impacting their ability to address customer issues promptly. By optimizing throughput and managing WIP effectively, they can reduce the overall number of support tickets and improve customer satisfaction.

Summary

In summary, this chapter of expert interviews has provided valuable insights into user stories and their effective implementation. Through in-depth interviews with industry experts – Sean Mack, Bob Galen, Michael Spayd, and Lyssa Adkins – we have gained a deeper understanding of the purpose and benefits of user stories, as well as practical tips and techniques for creating and refining them. The chapter has highlighted the importance of user-centricity, collaboration, and continuous improvement in the user story process.

The knowledge and skills described in this chapter are highly useful for anyone involved in Agile development or product management. By learning from experts and understanding their perspectives, you can enhance your ability to craft meaningful user stories, effectively communicate with stakeholders, and drive successful product development.

The next chapter will serve as a wrap-up and final reflection on the key concepts and learnings discussed throughout the book. It will provide a summary of the main topics covered, highlighting the importance of user stories in Agile development and product management.

The concluding chapter will serve as a final thought-provoking section, leaving you with a sense of accomplishment and motivation to apply your newfound knowledge and skills in your future endeavors.

Questions

1. What are the key takeaways from the expert interviews in this chapter?

2. How can you apply the lessons learned from these expert interviews in your own work?

Answers

1. The expert interviews in this chapter offer a wealth of knowledge and insights. Some key takeaways include the importance of clear communication and collaboration with stakeholders, the significance of empathy in understanding user needs, and the value of iterative and incremental development and the continuous improvement mindset. The interviews also highlight the significance of user feedback and prioritization and the role of user stories in driving product success.

2. You can apply the lessons learned from the expert interviews by incorporating the recommended strategies and best practices into your own Agile development processes. You can enhance your user story refinement techniques, improve stakeholder engagement, and adopt a mindset of continuous improvement. By leveraging the insights and experiences shared by the experts, you can refine your approach to user stories, enhance your collaboration with stakeholders, and drive the successful delivery of valuable products.

9

Conclusion

In this book, we have explored the world of user stories, delving into their significance and uncovering the best practices for creating effective user stories. We have seen how user stories serve as a powerful tool for capturing user needs, fostering collaboration, and driving the development of successful software products.

Throughout the chapters, we discussed the importance of user-centric thinking, the anatomy of a user story, managing stakeholder expectations, and the process of refining and prioritizing user stories. We explored various techniques and frameworks, such as MoSCoW, value-based prioritization, RICE, and the Kano model. We also examined the role of acceptance criteria and the definition of done in ensuring the quality and completeness of user stories.

We explored the role of user stories in agile development, emphasizing the iterative and collaborative nature of the process. We also discussed the significance of continuous improvement, stakeholder engagement, and effective communication in the successful implementation of user stories. Now, in this chapter, we will be sharing questions and answers related to what was discussed throughout this book.

How can user stories benefit the software development process?

User stories provide a clear and concise way of capturing user needs and translating them into product requirements. A focus on user needs will help us define a product that meets what a user needs and helps solve the user's problems. This leads to better alignment between the development team and the users, resulting in a higher likelihood of delivering a product that meets their needs.

What are some common challenges in writing effective user stories?

Writing effective user stories can be challenging, especially for those new to the process. Some common challenges include capturing the right level of detail, avoiding assumptions, identifying the user of the product, and prioritizing features. It's important to ensure that user stories are clear, specific, and actionable, while also being flexible enough to accommodate changes and iterations.

How can user stories be refined and improved over time?

User stories can be refined and improved through an iterative process. This involves continuously gathering feedback from users and stakeholders, revisiting and updating the acceptance criteria, and incorporating lessons learned from previous iterations. Regular refinement sessions and retrospectives help identify areas for improvement and ensure that user stories evolve to meet changing needs.

What role does stakeholder engagement play in the success of user stories?

Stakeholder engagement is crucial in the development and refinement of user stories. By actively involving stakeholders such as product owners, users, and management in the process, their perspectives and insights can be incorporated into the user stories. This ensures that the final product reflects their needs and goals, leading to higher user satisfaction and product success.

How can user stories help foster collaboration within a development team?

User stories act as a bridge between stakeholders and the development team. They provide a shared understanding of the requirements and serve as a basis for collaboration and communication. By breaking down the development process into smaller, manageable pieces, user stories allow the team to work together more effectively, align their efforts, and deliver value in each iteration.

What are some tips for successfully implementing user stories in an agile development environment?

To successfully implement user stories in an agile development environment, it is important to prioritize clear communication, collaboration, and continuous improvement. Some tips include involving stakeholders from the start, maintaining a backlog of user stories, regularly refining and prioritizing the backlog, and ensuring a shared understanding of acceptance criteria. It is also crucial to embrace an iterative approach, adapt to changing requirements, and foster a culture of learning and adaptation within the team.

How can user stories contribute to the overall success of a software product?

User stories play a vital role in the success of a software product by ensuring that the development team remains focused on delivering value to the end users. By capturing user needs and requirements, user stories guide the development process, aid in prioritization and decision-making, and provide a framework for testing, acceptance, and validation. They help drive customer satisfaction, reduce rework, and ultimately contribute to the delivery of a high-quality and user-centric software product.

Summary

Throughout the book, we provided concrete examples, case studies, and practical tips to help you navigate the complexities of user story development. We equipped you with the knowledge and skills necessary to create user stories that effectively capture user needs, guide the development process, and lead to the delivery of exceptional software products.

As you conclude your journey through this book, we encourage you to apply the concepts and techniques learned to your own products and organizations. Experiment, iterate, and refine your approach to user story development, always striving for continuous improvement. Embrace the user-centric mindset and foster a culture of collaboration and communication within your teams.

Remember that user stories are not just a tool but a mindset—a way of thinking that puts the user at the center of the development process. By empathizing with users, actively engaging stakeholders, and embracing the iterative nature of agile development, you can create products that truly meet user needs and drive customer satisfaction.

We hope that this book has provided you with valuable insights, practical guidance, and inspiration to embark on your user story journey. Embrace the power of user stories, and may your future endeavors be marked by successful product development, delighted users, and continuous growth.

Thank you for joining us on this exciting exploration of user stories. Best of luck on your journey!

- Christopher Lee

Index

www.packtpub.com

Subscribe to our online digital library for full access to over 7,000 books and videos, as well as industry leading tools to help you plan your personal development and advance your career. For more information, please visit our website.

Why subscribe?

- Spend less time learning and more time coding with practical eBooks and Videos from over 4,000 industry professionals

- Improve your learning with Skill Plans built especially for you

- Get a free eBook or video every month

- Fully searchable for easy access to vital information

- Copy and paste, print, and bookmark content

Did you know that Packt offers eBook versions of every book published, with PDF and ePub files available? You can upgrade to the eBook version at packtpub.com and as a print book customer, you are entitled to a discount on the eBook copy. Get in touch with us at customercare@packtpub.com for more details.

At www.packtpub.com, you can also read a collection of free technical articles, sign up for a range of free newsletters, and receive exclusive discounts and offers on Packt books and eBooks.

Other Books You May Enjoy

If you enjoyed this book, you may be interested in these other books by Packt:

Effective Platform Product Management

Tabassum Memon

ISBN: 9781801811354

- Understand the difference between the product and platform business model
- Build an end-to-end platform strategy from scratch
- Translate the platform strategy to a roadmap with a well-defined implementation plan
- Define the MVP for faster releases and test viability in the early stages
- Create an operating model and design an execution plan
- Measure the success or failure of the platform and make iterations after feedback

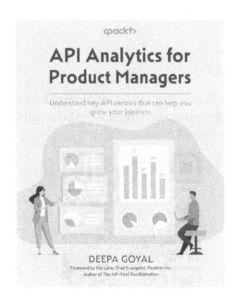

API Analytics for Product Managers

Deepa Goyal

ISBN: 9781803247656

- Build a long-term strategy for an API
- Explore the concepts of the API life cycle and API maturity
- Understand APIs from a product management perspective
- Create support models for your APIs that scale with the product
- Apply user research principles to APIs
- Explore the metrics of activation, retention, engagement, and churn
- Cluster metrics together to provide context
- Examine the consequences of gameable and vanity metrics

Packt is searching for authors like you

If you're interested in becoming an author for Packt, please visit `authors.packtpub.com` and apply today. We have worked with thousands of developers and tech professionals, just like you, to help them share their insight with the global tech community. You can make a general application, apply for a specific hot topic that we are recruiting an author for, or submit your own idea.

Share Your Thoughts

Now you've finished *The Art of Crafting User Stories*, we'd love to hear your thoughts! Scan the QR code below to go straight to the Amazon review page for this book and share your feedback or leave a review on the site that you purchased it from.

https://packt.link/r/1837639493

Your review is important to us and the tech community and will help us make sure we're delivering excellent quality content.

Download a free PDF copy of this book

Thanks for purchasing this book!

Do you like to read on the go but are unable to carry your print books everywhere?

Is your eBook purchase not compatible with the device of your choice?

Don't worry, now with every Packt book you get a DRM-free PDF version of that book at no cost.

Read anywhere, any place, on any device. Search, copy, and paste code from your favorite technical books directly into your application.

The perks don't stop there, you can get exclusive access to discounts, newsletters, and great free content in your inbox daily

Follow these simple steps to get the benefits:

1. Scan the QR code or visit the link below

https://packt.link/free-ebook/9781837639496

2. Submit your proof of purchase
3. That's it! We'll send your free PDF and other benefits to your email directly

www.ingramcontent.com/pod-product-compliance
Lightning Source LLC
Chambersburg PA
CBHW060131060326
40690CB00018B/3834